ConcentricCoaching™

The Concentric Coaching System™

by

Brian P. O'Brien, MMC, PCC

The **CCS**™ is a systematic coaching model which is compatible with all of the top coaching schools in the U.S. and is a proven methodology for both the new and experienced coach!!

The Concentric Coaching System™
is a product of
Myriad Performance Services, Inc.

For more information contact:

Brian P. O'Brien at 301-682-8382

For additional information or for permission to use material from this text or product, submit a request online at Brian@Myriad-PSI.com.

Trademarks
Concentric Coaching: A Systematic Coaching Model™ and the Concentric Coaching *MAP*™ is a trademark of Myriad Performance Services, Inc. Some of the product names used in this book have been used for identification purposes only, and may be trademarked or registered trademarks of their respective manufacturer and sellers.

Disclaimer
Myriad Performance Services, Inc. reserves the right to revise this publication and make changes from time to time in its content without notice.

ISBN:1-4392-4141-4
Library of Congress Catalogue Card Number pending

TABLE OF CONTENTS

ABOUT THE AUTHOR

Mr. Brian P. O'Brien

Brian is the President of Myriad Performance Services, Inc. Myriad is an international training, coaching, and consulting firm located in Frederick, Maryland.

Brian has a BS in engineering/management and an MA/ISD from UMBC and has completed projects ranging from being an examiner for the U.S. Senate Productivity and Maryland Quality Awards (National Baldrige Program) to the design of the training system used by the Eastern European nuclear industries.

Additionally, he has provided training and development services to finance, manufacturing, health care, and the US government. Since 2003, Brian has been actively working as a coach and mentor for international business clients.

Brian has completed the Graduate School of Coaching program with Coachville. Additionally, Brian has completed all certification requirements as a Master Mentor Coach (MMC) and the ICF Professional Coach Certification (PCC).

INTRODUCTION

We have all wanted more...or less....of something. More time at home, less difficulty with those with whom we work. Or perhaps we feel a need for something different. We just don't know how to express what we want or, if we do, how to get to the desired outcome.

But we already know that. It's not that we don't know what we want; we just don't know how to <u>ask</u> for what we want. And many coaches aren't that skilled in finding out what a client wants as well. To a large extent, it's a matter of mindset...a matter of language...a matter of thinking.

What is needed is a <u>new way</u> of thinking.

In the last ten years, coaching has been the subject of many books. Training organizations and even colleges have started offering coaching education. Most programs provide excellent skills vital to the change process; but, like any new discipline, it takes time for the supporting materials to mature into a universally accepted process. What has been missing is a *concrete vocabulary and methodology* to describe and explain the coaching process. This problem with the deficiency in languaging and communication skills has resulted in a wide range of schools trying to teach skills...without a common process. Additionally, there is a large gap between the books which have been written, the training which has been provided, and the skills needed to provide an effective...and valuable....coaching conversation. This is evident in the small percentage of applicants who pass the written and demonstration portions of many of the coaching certifiers.

The Concentric Coaching System: A Systematic Coaching Model™ (**CCS**™) is designed to resolve that exact problem!! **CCS**™ is designed to help new coaches understand the high level logic and functional process steps of moving a prospective client through the coaching conversation. However, a text isn't the best method to use during an actual coaching conversation; so, to support the translation of the text to functional conversation, we designed the

CCS™ **MAP**™. The **MAP**™ provides a visual aid for moving through the model. Take a look at the **MAP**™ provided to familiarize yourself with the structure and design of the diagram.

While the **CCS**™ book provides the theoretical foundation for learning how to be become a more powerful coach, the **MAP**™ can reveal a missed process step for the experienced coach who occasionally finds themselves stuck in their conversation with a client.

Additionally, the model is designed to accommodate the processes of every school that we were able to contact…because it is <u>outcome</u> based and doesn't challenge the methodologies provided by the schools. However, it <u>does</u> provide the vocabulary for the coaching experience…..whether you are a spiritual, holistic, corporate, or life coach.

This process can work for you!!

HOW TO USE THIS BOOK

This book is all about making *The Concentric Coaching System: A Systematic Coaching Model*™ (*CCS*™) easy to use for the new and experienced coach.

After much thought, we recommend the following strategy for blending the *CCS*™ system with the tools you bring to coaching:

1. Review the **CCS**™ **MAP**™ on page 10 or <u>under</u> the cover of the book cover. The **MAP**™ is the cornerstone of the process. Take a look at the **MAP**™, review each Building Block (the large brown boxes on top of the segments), and make sure that it makes sense to you.

2. Next, read the entire book very quickly. Get an overview of the process. Keep the **MAP**™ in front of you as you read the book and routinely compare the **MAP**™ with what is being said in the book.

3. Then, back up and reread each segment in the book <u>very</u> carefully. As you are reading each segment, envision how you might apply these techniques to your current coaching practice. Think of the questions that you might ask. See if the questions we provide are the best for your particular style and conversation. Consider the input and output to each segment and validate <u>our</u> suggestions to what <u>you</u> think is appropriate and reasonable.

4. Finally, once you think you have a concrete view of what each segment can do for your coaching conversation, select the first segment, WANTS, and apply just that one segment to your next coaching conversation. See if the input and output doesn't make your client's goals and desires more clear. As you master one segment, move to the next segment, MOTIVATION, and now apply both WANTS and MOTIVATION to your next coaching conversation. Continue this way, until you have integrated ALL of the eleven (11) segments into your coaching conversation

We believe this process…combined with the tools you have brought to the table from your coaching school….will make you a stronger, more confident…and certainly a more organized coach.

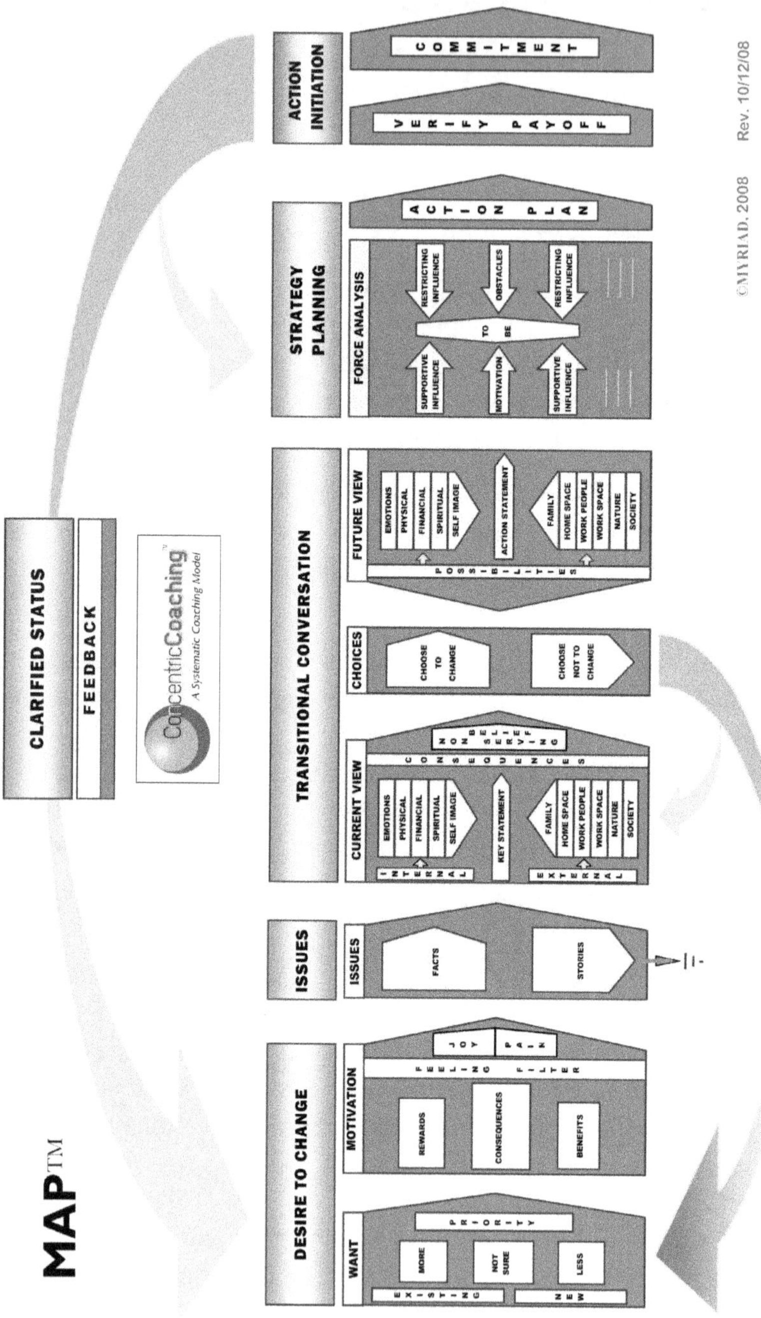
MAP™
CLARIFIED STATUS
FEEDBACK
ConcentricCoaching
A Systematic Coaching Model
DESIRE TO CHANGE
WANT
EXISTING
NEW
MORE
NOT SURE
LESS
PRIORITY
MOTIVATION
REWARDS
CONSEQUENCES
BENEFITS
FEELING FILTER
JOY
PAIN
ISSUES
ISSUES
FACTS
STORIES
TRANSITIONAL CONVERSATION
CURRENT VIEW
INTERNAL
EMOTIONS
PHYSICAL
FINANCIAL
SPIRITUAL
SELF IMAGE
KEY STATEMENT
EXTERNAL
FAMILY
HOME SPACE
WORK PEOPLE
WORK SPACE
NATURE
SOCIETY
CONSEQUENCES
CHOICES
CHOOSE TO CHANGE
CHOOSE NOT TO CHANGE
FUTURE VIEW
POSSIBILITIES
EMOTIONS
PHYSICAL
FINANCIAL
SPIRITUAL
SELF IMAGE
ACTION STATEMENT
FAMILY
HOME SPACE
WORK PEOPLE
WORK SPACE
NATURE
SOCIETY
STRATEGY PLANNING
FORCE ANALYSIS
SUPPORTIVE INFLUENCE
MOTIVATION
SUPPORTIVE INFLUENCE
TO BE
RESTRICTING INFLUENCE
OBSTACLES
RESTRICTING INFLUENCE
ACTION PLAN
ACTION INITIATION
VERIFY PAYOFF
COMMITMENT
©MYRIAD, 2008
Rev. 10/12/08

BUILDING BLOCKS

The Concentric Coaching System (**CCS**™) is different than a traditional coaching model in that, although it does have a starting point, it really doesn't have an ending point. It's circular. More specifically, it's concentric; moving the client consistently toward a new, desired behavior.

As mentioned before, the **CCS**™ is illustrated by the **MAP**™. Use the **MAP**™ and follow along with the next discussion.

As you review the **MAP**™ you will notice that it is made up of a series of blocks illustrating the high level logic or building blocks of the **CCS**™ process.

Each building block expands down, similar to a computer drop-down menu, into the various segments. You will notice that each segment is a different color for ease of identification. There may be more than one segment for each building block.

The following is a <u>brief</u> explanation of each of the six (6) building blocks of the **CCS**™ model. Later in the book, each segment will be fully explored.

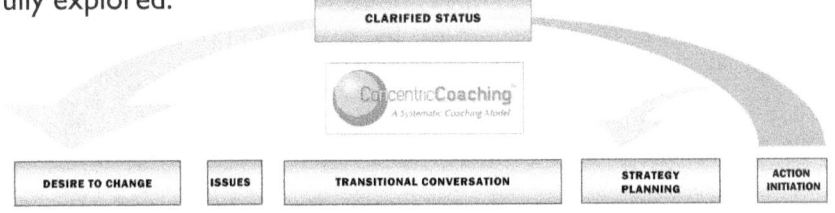

There are six (6) Building Blocks

1. **Desire to Change**
2. **Issues**
3. **Transitional Conversation**
4. **Strategy Planning**
5. **Action Initiation and**
6. **Clarified Status**

11

1. Starting from the left side of the **MAP**™, the building block, Desire to Change is the launching point for the process. It is during this part of the conversation that the client's wants and motivations are identified.

2. The client's want is then processed through the ISSUES building block. This is where the facts and stories contained within the client's wants are identified, developed, and processed….and sometimes eliminated.

3. The next building block is the core of the **CCS**™; the Transitional Conversation. This conversation directs the client through an exploration of what is, making a choice to consider change, then mirror-imaging into developing the vision of what the client could become. This stage of the conversation is the core of coaching and the **CCS**™ process.

4. Once a decision has been made and the new vision established, it's time for Strategy Planning. In the Strategy Planning building block a force analysis is conducted and an action plan is constructed. A force analysis is a graphical illustration of the forces competing to support and oppose the client in meeting their desire. The ACTION PLAN is the process of moving the client from their current view to the realization of their future view…in a very real sense. Not just hopes and dreams…but fully and completely meeting the goal.

5. Once the action plan has been constructed, it's time for action with the Action Initiation building block. This block is where the payoff is verified and the commitment to the client's action plan is made. If you don't know why you should meet your goal…it's tough to sustain the energy necessary to reach that goal. And, you have to commit. You have to determine the cost of reaching your goal…then pay the price….willingly.

6. This might seem like the end of the action process, but the **CCS**™ **MAP**™ continues the process…a concentric process…moving into the Clarified Status building block. In this block, feedback from the client is processed to determine how the client is doing on their action plan and whether or not a

new want is warranted. Is the client moving smoothly toward their desire? Is the client ready for a break or a new want?

7. Finally, the client finds themselves back at the Desire to Change building block - completing the entire **concentric** coaching conversation!!

8. For an example of a coaching conversation, refer to the Coaching Conversations later starting on page 134.

SEGMENTS

A highly experienced coach, having been trained in all of the tools necessary to provide competent services, may well be able to move through all of the six (6) building blocks without additional support. However, we have found that visual aids help facilitate a flexible, and reliable roadmap for the coaching conversation. Thus, the segment.

Segments drill down one level below the building blocks to support the coaching conversation. Segments, as represented on the **MAP**™, provide the coach with a visual support system for completing each building block.

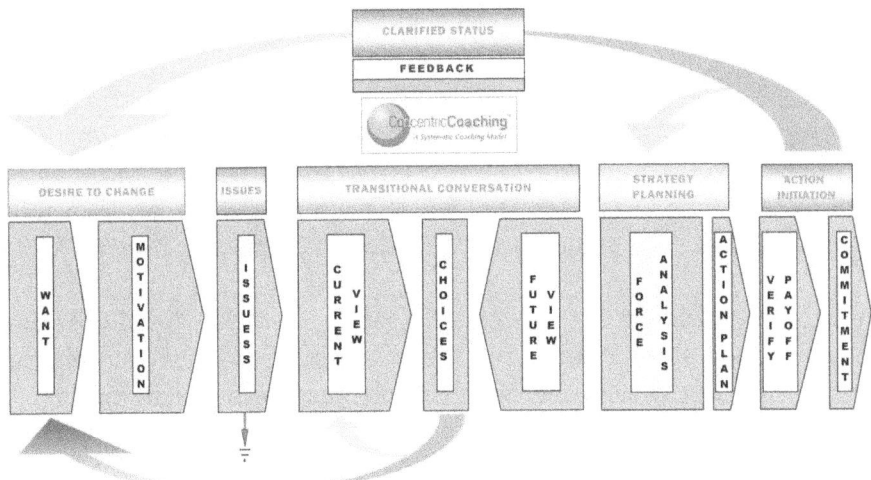

For example, with the first building block, Desire to Change, there are two segments: WANT and MOTIVATION. The completion of the WANT segment establishes the priority to which the client assigns their desire or goal. The completion of the *MOTIVATION* segment helps the client determine if their goal is driven by the desire to enlarge themselves through joy (i.e., the want of more time with a spouse) or to stabilize themselves by removing pain (i.e., removing themselves from a self-destructive relationship). Working through the segments...in order... helps the coach move the client one step closer to the achievement of their goal or desire.

Successful completion of a segment means to have reached the desired outcome for that segment. We'll talk more about each segment and their respective outcomes shortly.

BUT....sometimes the segments just aren't sufficient. What if the coach needs even more support through the coaching process? What could be developed to support that need?

GUIDES

We came up with "guides" to help the coach move the client from the input of the segment to the outcome of each segment. A guide is represented on the **MAP**™ as small grey or white boxes within each segment.
Each guide within the segment is unique to that segment and is used to help the coach drill down even farther during the coaching conversation.

When you were new at coaching, did you ever worry about what you were going to say...and why? All you needed were guideposts to help. Well, the guides illustrated within each segment provide exactly that assistance. The guides help remind the coach what to ask next.

Remember, coaching is a process....regardless of the type of coaching and the needs of the client...and the process needs guides to help the coach figure out what to do next. Guides help with exactly that dilemma.

Take a look at the **MAP**™ to see guides. For example, in the Desire to Change building block and in the *WANT* segment, there are actually six (6) guides:

14

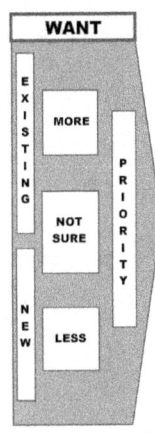

Existing – is the desire an existing/working desire?

New – is the desire or goal new?

More – does the client want more of something?

Less – does the client want less of something?

Not sure – or is the client unsure of what they want?

Priority - And finally, of all of the client's desires…which is the highest priority?

In the Transition Conversation building block, *CURRENT VIEW* segment there are as many as <u>16</u> guides. It depends on the depth of the conversation and complexity of the segment as to how many guides are needed.

As always, review the **MAP**™ to see all of the types of guides there are within each of the segments.

Although completion of <u>all</u> of the guides within a segment isn't necessary, the experienced coach will notice that a thread will form between the guides; connecting one thought to another throughout the coaching conversation. Take a look at the coaching conversation at the end of the book for an example of this threading process.

Each guide within each segment will be covered in greater detail in the segments to come.

OUTCOMES

An outcome is the consequence or result from each segment. The beauty of this methodology is that the outcomes are specific to the segment, not to the topic. An outcome is a concrete statement or conclusion reached through a process of logical thought. It doesn't matter what the subject matter is. It doesn't matter who the client is.

It doesn't matter whether your coaching is corporate, spiritual, or gardening. The truth of the matter is....if the segments work for you....the outcomes will too.

As just described, an outcome is the consequence of a process of logical thought. Three requirements of a process are:

An <u>input</u>...<u>processing</u> of that input...and an <u>output.</u>

As an example of an outcome from the *WANT* segment:

> The **input** is the information that the client brings to the conversation. In the case of the first segment, *WANT*, the client brings a <u>desire to change</u>. This is the starting point for any coaching conversation and the input to the *WANT* segment.
>
> The coaching conversation...is the **process**. The right questions asked, the observations, the careful listening....all of these are part of the process.
>
> The **output** of the *WANT* segment is <u>a prioritized want</u>, a specified desire to accomplish something. The answer to the question..."So, what shall we talk about today"!!

For a listing of all of the inputs and output (consequences) for each segment, see the chapter on each respective segment to follow.

QUESTIONS/INQUIRY

In the previous section, it was mentioned that the process was the engine of the coaching experience. This engine is fueled by effective questioning techniques used by the coach. From the coaching side of the equation, the question is paramount in the coaching conversation.

But which question....when? What is the vocabulary that the effective coach might use to talk with another coach or a client? How might coaches communicate without getting into "coach speak"?

How might you develop or generate the perfect question…and (horror of horrors) remember it? And how would you be able to develop the "perfect question" for each of six building blocks….eleven segments….a greater number of guides…multitudes of clients….lions and tigers and bears, OH MY!!

While an experienced coach might have no problem using the **MAP**™ to move through the coaching process, the novice or learning coach might need help upon occasion remembering the perfect question for each segment. At the same time, you don't want to interrupt your live call with your client to read through a handout or manual to find the question. This is where the **CCS**™ model really shines!

As you look through each segment in their respective chapters to follow, you will notice that there is a page with a table containing a series of abbreviated questions. The table is made up of six (6) boxes. There are two process boxes, labeled input and output, located through the middle of the tables and four quadrants splitting the table into four large boxes.

The input box illustrates what the client brings to this segment of the model. The output box describes what the client needs to do prior to exiting this segment. The input and output is specified here to aid the coach in remembering what the segment is trying to elicit from the client – at a glance.

The top left quadrant is the **Support Leading** box. This area contains the questions designed to support, rather than challenge, the client while leading them through the process.

The bottom left quadrant is the **Obstacle Leading** box. This area contains the questions designed to challenge the client while leading them through the process.

Similarly, the top right quadrant is the **Support Bridging** box. This area contains the questions designed to provide a supportive attitude while bridging the process to the desired, indicated outcome.

And finally, the bottom right quadrant is the **Obstacle <u>Bridging</u>** box. This area contains the questions designed to cause the client to verify their intent with regard to this segment. Do they really want to move to the next step; is the support structure there, is it the right time.....if so, then let's get to it!!

You will also notice that each quadrant has three (3) questions which support the process for that quadrant...providing you with the stimulus for the best question...without having to wonder where that question is located.

But, what do we mean by *stimulus?* As you have looked through the table, you may have noticed that the questions are abbreviated....or shortened. We call these abbreviated questions: Question Tips or "Q-tips". A Q-tip is a hint as to what your question could be. You KNOW the right question...you just need a little reminder or nudge. The Q-TIPs provide that nudge.

This tabular format is designed specifically to permit the coach to:

1. Quickly go to the right quadrant (depending on whether you want to lead or bridge)

2. Reliably know that the right question is there waiting for you and finally,

3. Precisely know the desired outcome for this particular segment...consistent with the needs and desires of each unique and individual client.

When you are just learning how to coach, you may not know exactly what to ask at any particular moment...especially given the vast array of possible clients. AND, the Q-TIPs may not make sense yet. Don't worry; we'll expand on each of the Q-TIPs in their respective Segment Chapters to follow.

CONTENTS OF EACH SEGMENT/CHAPTER

The next series of chapters examine each and every single building block, segment, guide, input, output, and Q-TIP for all of the eleven segments.

The chapters review each segment following the flowpath of the *MAP*™:

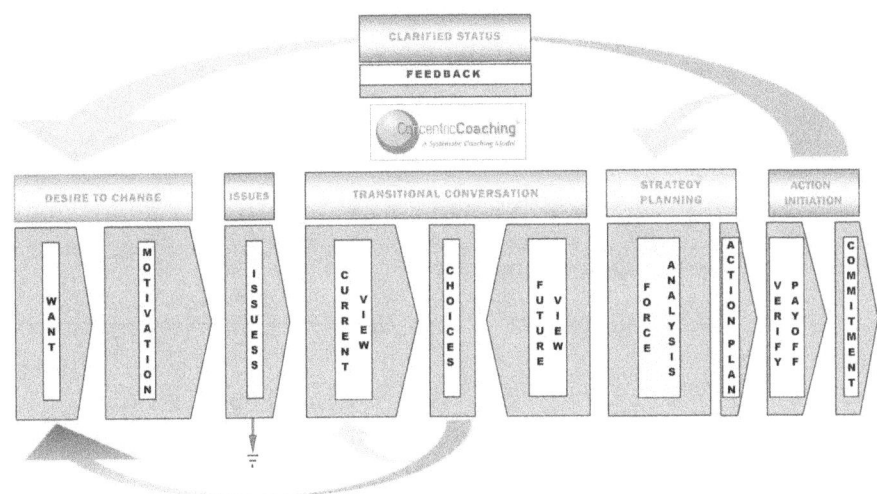

Segment 1: Desire to Change: Want

Segment 2: Desire to Change: Motivation

Segment 3: Issues: Issues

Segment 4: Transitional Conversation: Current View

Segment 5: Transitional Conversation: Choices

Segment 6: Transitional Conversation: Future View

Segment 7: Strategy Planning: Force Analysis

Segment 8: Strategy Planning: Action Plan

Segment 9: Action Initiation: Verify Payoff

Segment 10: Action Initiation: Commitment

Segment 11: Clarified Status: Feedback

Each chapter or segment is organized in the same sequence so you know exactly where to find what you are looking for.

Each segment contains:

1. The Segment Cover Page
2. The Question Page (Q-tips and Outcome)
3. The Training & Discussion Pages, containing
   a. Purpose of the Segment
   b. Input
   c. Output
   d. Guides
   e. Definitions, and
   f. Questions

The Training & Discussion pages are particularly important to the new coach. Every single important word used in the model is explained. This may seem like overkill, but the truth of the matter is….so much about coaching is assumed. We decided that if we were going to use a word, we wanted it operatively defined. You may not want to savor every morsel provided to you. But, on the other hand, if you don't know what something means…we provide a definition of EVERYTHING.

To summarize, the **CCS**™ model will allow you to seamlessly find your way to the right segment in the manual….with the input and output clearly specified….with appropriate supportive or challenging abbreviated questions

So, without further ado….please turn the page to begin to use the easiest coaching manual in print: the

Concentric Coaching System™ !!

SEGMENT 1: WANT

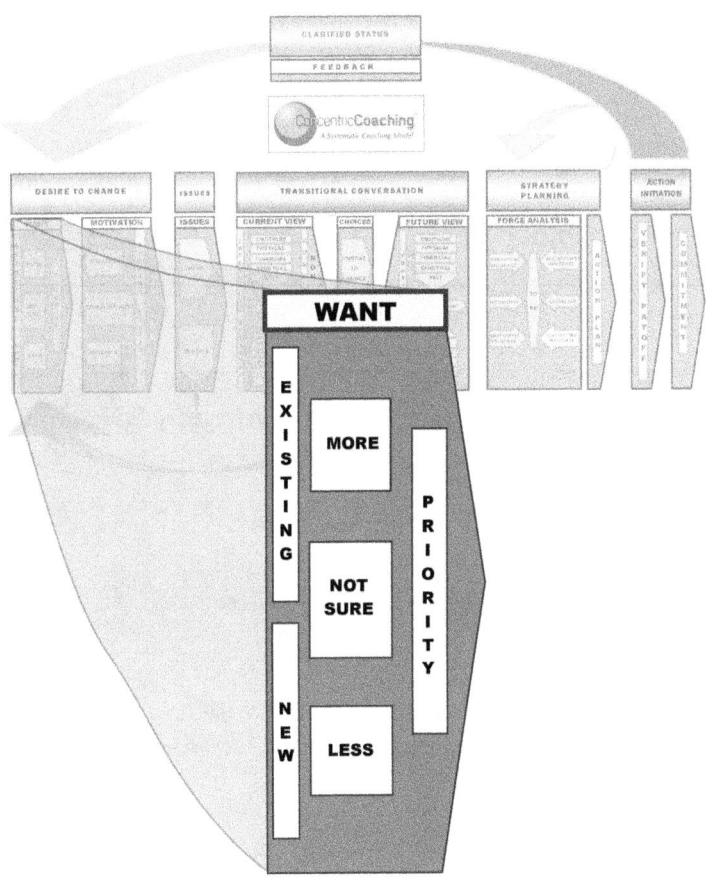

Table of Q-TIP Questions

Support Leading	Support Bridging
1. What talk about today? 2. Last week's assignment? 3. More of that?	7. Which is highest priority? 8. Why a priority? 9. What did you learn from that?
Input *Desire to change* ⇨	*Output* *Prioritized want* ⇨
4. Less of that? 5. Struggling to get focused? 6. A lot on your plate...why today?	10. Actual want or symptom? 11. Why want more? 12. Why want less?
Obstacle Leading	**Obstacle Bridging**

Intention of the Q-tips for this segment:

This segment is all about identifying the goal, desire....or want....of the client.

The **Input** is the desired change; the client with a new want might have an idea what they want, but may not have identified it concretely.

The **Output** of this segment is a prioritized want; the client now knows what they want...but may not even know why.

SEGMENT 1: WANT
Training & Discussion

1. Purpose of the Segment

a.   The purpose of this segment is to provide the client with a framework within which to focus their intent. Clients enter the coaching process in either of four mind sets: (1) They want more of something, (2) They want less of something, or (3) They are unfocused. Lastly, if the client is working on an existing action plan, (4) Continue the current action plan.

b.   An example of a client wanting more of something might be... "I'd like more attention from my wife" or "I'd like to be promoted" or "I need to increase my income by 10% in the next quarter". In these cases, it is clear that the client wants more of something. Sometimes the want-more-of is a bit more subtle. For example, a client might say that they'd like to spend less time at work; however, upon examination, what the client wants is more attention or approval from their spouse.

c.   An example of a client wanting less of something might be "I would like to spend less time at work" or "I would like less stress in my life" or "I'd like to have more focus (less confusion)".

d.   If the client has no idea what they want to talk about during this session, the coach needs to help the client differentiate between (1) not having a goal, (2) knowing generally, but not specifically, what is desired, or (3) knowing what they want, but having no idea how to get it.

e.   Finally, the input from the feedback loop, suggests a need for status update from what was committed to during the last coaching session. How is the action plan working, does anything need to be adjusted or corrected? Or is it time for a new (or an old, forgotten) want?

2. **Input**

   a.   The input in the **Concentric Coaching System**™ model is the de*sired change* and comes from one of two sources: a new want or a want-to-continue the conversation about an existing action plan.

   b.   Without the desire to change, coaching will NOT take place. You cannot force a client to begin to change.

   c.   However, you <u>can</u> help a client arrive at a topic or situation which the client might consider changing. Sometimes in the course of the conversation, a particular issue or aspect of a person's life might be worth changing....once they become aware of it. However, as always, it must be the client's agenda....not the coach's agenda.

3. **Output**

   a.   The output of the first segment of the **Concentric Coaching System**™ model is a prioritized want.

   b.   The topic should be clear, attainable, and relevant to the client...and within their control.

   c.   Through the course of discussion, the client may bring up a number of issues or topics which might meet the criteria of being clear, attainable, and relevant....however, given the brief nature of the conversation, only one topic at a time should be examined.

   d.   Therefore, the client needs to identify the one topic in which to begin the discussion. It should be noted that frequently the issue or topic which progresses through the entire model is NOT the originally selected topic. It is not uncommon to have an issue surface which becomes a higher priority. The point of the output of this segment of the model is that it should be clear to both the coach and the client exactly what they are working on at any point in the conversation.

4. Guides

a.   The small boxes and other shapes within the segments are called "guides". An example of guides in the first segment, *WANT*, are the boxes labeled More, Not Sure, Less, and Priority.

b.   Guides provide a pathway for the coach to identify those aspects of the conversation that will guide you from the input to the output.

c.   In the example of the *WANT* segment of the model, the coach will guide the client through identifying if they want more of something, less of something....then prioritizing what they actually want to talk about in order to arrive at the end point...the prioritized want.

d.   Some of the segments have fairly complex guides. In the case of the *CURRENT VIEW* segment there are a number of guides. In this case, the coach is looking for a key statement that will trigger the client to more carefully examining their beliefs. Additionally, the client will be moving through an examination of internal or external environments during that discussion. The coach and the client will examine the consequences of those beliefs in an effort to arrive at the root cause or source of a particular non-serving belief.

5. Definitions

(Coach's Note: in the first segment, we will cover every single word in <u>excruciating</u> detail; however, every subsequent definition section will get smaller and less detailed.)

a. **Concentric Coaching System**™ model: **CCS**™ is the process of supporting the client through the inputs and outputs of each segment and building block in order to (1) identify exactly what the client REALLY wants to achieve, (2) develop a vision of what achieving that want will look like, and (3) construction of a clear plan on how to achieve that want.

b. Process vs. Rule: A process is one way of doing a particular task. A rule is *the* way of doing a particular task. The **Concentric Coaching System**™ model specifies just one way of moving from an input to an output without demanding the way in which it's done. The model suggests a way...and you are quite welcome to modify the way in which the process is done as long as the outcome is met.

c. Segment: A segment is one step in the **Concentric Coaching System**™ model. There are a total of eleven (11) segments in this model each containing a number of guides. The segments provide a methodology which will assist the coach in moving the client from one outcome to another progressing to a client-formulated plan.

d. Guide: A guide is a placeholder within a segment which describes the sub-steps within a larger segment.

e. Input, Process, Output: The input is a behavior, belief, or position held by a client prior to a change. The Process indicates a methodology for consideration of change by the client. The output is the result of their change in position or belief. You may notice that the output of one segment is the same (approximately) as the input to the subsequent segment.

f. Questions: The questions are provided to aid the new coach in identifying a potentially relevant question. They are also helpful to the experienced coach during a momentary lapse in identifying the best question for that moment/segment. Questions are designed specifically for each segment and provided in the four quadrants of the page to facilitate the coach in finding the more relevant question for the moment. The quadrants include support leading, obstacle leading, support bridging, and obstacle bridging Q-Tip questions.

g. Support Leading: A support leading question is a question that a coach might ask a client, which clarifies the beliefs or desires of the client about the segment process. The question leads the client through the process. The support aspect of the question indicates a more supportive position by the coach rather than a challenging or provocative position by the coach.

h. Support Bridging: A support bridging question is a question which a coach might ask a client which moves the client through the segment process to the desired outcome. The question "bridges" the client to the outcome in preparation for the next segment of the model.

i. Obstacle Leading: An obstacle leading question is a question that a coach might ask a client which clarifies the obstacles or inhibitions the client might be experiencing at that segment process. The question leads the client through the process. The obstacle aspect of the question indicates a more challenging or provocative position by the coach rather than a more supporting position by the coach.

j. Obstacle Bridging: An obstacle bridging question is a question which a coach might ask a client which moves the client through the segment process to the desired outcome. The question bridges the obstacles the client might be bringing to the outcome of the next segment of the model.

k. Q-tip: A "Q-tip" is an abbreviated question which stimulates the coach to ask a more fully stated question which is relevant to the place in the model. The reason for the abbreviated nature of the question is that it is desired that the coach stay engaged with the client and not have to (1) read through a full question to decide if it's even the right question and (2) adjust a full question to make it relevant to the client and the situation at hand. The Q-tip provides just enough of a question to allow the coach to find it quickly in the appropriate quadrant and rapidly adjust the question.

l.   Building Blocks: The building blocks represent the high level logic making up the **Concentric Coaching System** (**CCS**™). As referred to earlier, the building blocks house all of the segments.

m.   WANT: The *WANT* segment, located in the Desire to Change building block, is a stated desire for something to be different. Specifying a client's wants is the first and most important step in building a better life for a client. If the client can't determine what they want, then there is literally nothing to work on. All that's left is story telling. Story telling is all about symptoms and not about the root cause of a problem or opportunity. A client may list a number of wants and desires; however, since there is typically limited time to discuss the issue within a coaching session, it is important to establish a priority within the wants and desires of the client.

n.   Existing: Existing implies a continuation of the conversation from a previous coaching session.

o.   New: New implies a first time client or an existing client who has indicated a new want.

p.   More: More indicates a client who wants <u>more</u> of what they want. An example might be: "I want more time with my family".

q.   Less: The client has indicated that he/she wants less of their want. An example might be: "I want to spend less time at work being unproductive".

r.   Not Sure: The client is blocked, stuck, or unsure about what they want. They know they want to make a change, but they are having a difficulty expressing the concrete desire.

s.   Priority: The priority of which issue or opportunity to work on is exclusively the responsibility of the client. Although it is not uncommon for the discussion to move from one aspect of the issue to another (actually from one belief to another), the client alone can identify what he/she wants to work on during any given session. In the event that there is more than one thing that the client would like to discuss, it is up to the client to select which topic (a prioritized want) the conversation should be centered around.

(Coach's Note: Capture all of the issues which the client wants for use in subsequent discussions.)

6.   Questions

SUPPORT LEADING

Q-tip #1:   What talk about today?

Expanded question #1: So, what would you like to talk about today?

Discussion #1: This is one of many introductory, conversation starting questions. Another example might be "What have you been working on this past week?".

Q-tip #2:   Last week's assignment?

Expanded question #2: How did you do with the action plan from the last session/last week?
Discussion #2: If the actions went ok, are there any other actions we need to continue talking about? If no additional actions, then look for a new topic. An example of a similar question might be "Did you have any problems with the assignment from last week?"

Q-tip #3:   More of that?

Expanded question #3: Would you like more of that (whatever topic the client indicates)?

Discussion #3: In this case, the client has indicated wanting more of something. An example might be that the client wants more time with family.

OBSTACLE LEADING

Q-tip #4:   Less of that?

Expanded question #4: Would you like less of that?
Discussion #4: In this case, the client has indicated wanting less of something. An example might be that the client wants to spend less time at work..

Q-tip #5:   Struggling to get focused?

Expanded question #5: You seem to be struggling with what you want to talk about today...are you struggling to get focused....do you know what you want to talk about today?

Discussion #5: This situation is one in which the client may have so many potential issues, they can't even decide what to talk about today. The client might be overwhelmed with the complexity in their life at that moment. In this situation, the coach might share topics brought up in the past; "These were topics you brought up in the past, would one of these be important to work on today?" If the client doesn't really want to talk about what you just brought up...put the conversation back on the client.... "So, what shall we do today?" The client needs to take responsibility for the session. Sometimes (VERY infrequently) the client just needs to vent.

Q-tip #6:   A lot on your plate...why today?

Expanded question #6: "You seem like you have a lot on your plate today...that there is a lot going on.....why today? What makes today so different from other days?"

Discussion #6: The client is typically very focused, but finds themselves unfocused today. This question is all about why this day...and why they are normally more focused...what is happening today to make them unclear.

Q-tip #7:   Which is highest priority?

Expanded question #7: Those are all good and important candidate topics…which are the top three….which is the top one?

Discussion #7: In this situation, the client may have a lot on their mind; however the client needs to focus on exactly what they really want. The process of moving the client from multiple topics down to <u>their</u> one topic helps the client refocus and reestablish their priorities.

Q-tip #8:   Why a priority?

Expanded question #8: Why is that topic a priority over the others?

Discussion #8: This is a clarifying question. The question the coach is asking is used to more clearly understand why this particular topic is the most important. The hope is that resolving this one issue will help resolve a number of other lesser issues that are on the client's mind.

Q-tip #9:   What did you learn from that?

Expanded question #9: Now that you have identified the desired output, what did you learn from that…about yourself…about your capabilities? How can you use this new information in the future?

Discussion #9: This is a question which can be asked at the end of each segment. It is important to the client to acknowledge any moment of awareness or achievement…and why that awareness/achievement is important. This will permit the client to transport this new skill of realization to other opportunities throughout the process. The real question is….what did the client learn that is unique to this segment?

Q-tip #10   Actual want or a symptom?

Expanded Question #10: There seems to be more to what you are saying…are you talking about a want…or a symptom? Is there more that we need to look at or discuss?

Discussion #10: This might be viewed as a fairly abrupt question to the client; however, the point of the question is to cause the client to take a hard look at whether the issue at hand is the root cause of the situation or is the topic an illustration or symptom of a larger issue. This can be a delicate moment as well. If the client believes it's the root cause problem…then go with it. If it's a symptom, that will surface later in the discussion.

Q-tip #11:   Why want more?

Expanded Question #11: Why do you want more of that? What will that do for you?

Discussion #11: Asking this question is all about emotions rather than problem solving. The point of the question is to determine if the client actually wants more of what is being discussed or has a higher agenda. For example, if the client wants more money from work, a larger issue might be that the client is actually having trouble managing their income, the client may have lost control of their spending habits, there might be a change in a family situation (such as a child going to college) or it might be a repositioning of worth of the client at work. The point is that it's important for both the coach and the client to understand why more is important in order to facilitate the development of an effective strategy.

Q-tip #12:   Why want less?

Expanded Question #12: Why would you want less of that (the prioritized item proposed by client)?

Discussion #12: This question is about the emotion of the want; why does the client want less of something?

SEGMENT 2: MOTIVATION

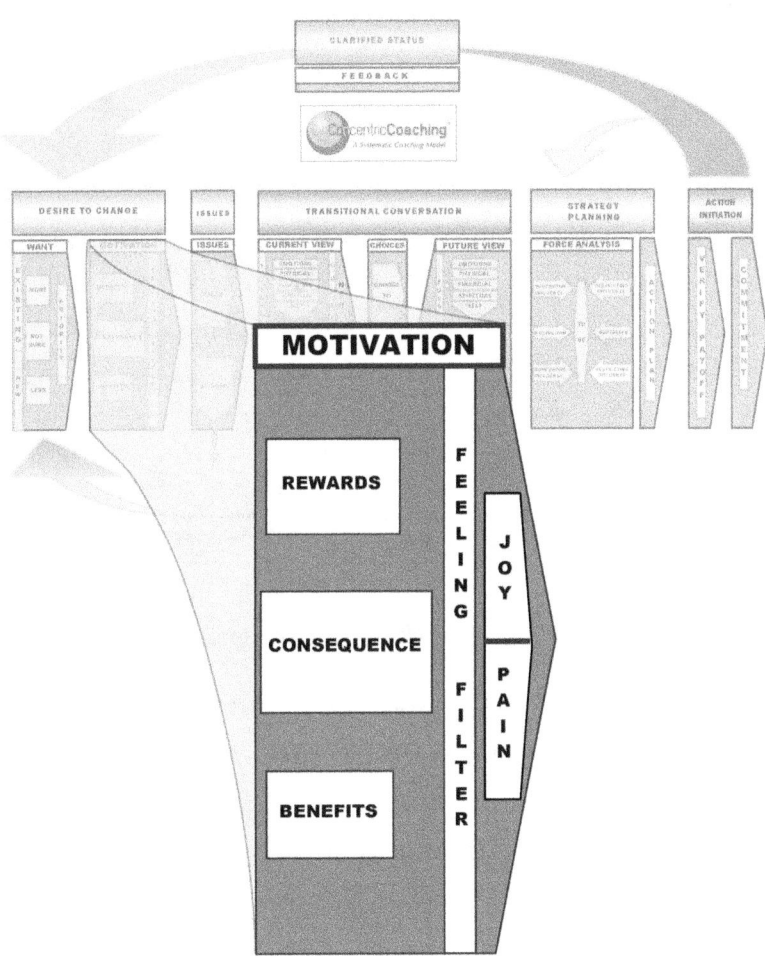

Table of Q-TIP Questions

Support Leading		Support Bridging	
1. Why important? 2. What are benefits? 3. Why want more?		7. What feelings does this bring up? 8. Does that bring joy? 9. What did you learn from that?	
Input *Prioritized Want*	⇨	*Output* *Filtered topic resulting in less pain & more joy*	⇨
4. Why want less? 5. Consequence of no change? 6. Is there anything else?		10. Anything stopping you? 11. What if it didn't work? 12. Will this reduce your pain?	
Obstacle Leading		**Obstacle Bridging**	

Intention of the Q-Tips for this segment:

This segment is all about motivation; filtering the prioritized want through the client's values in order to arrive at the topic which will lessen pain and increase joy.

The **Input** is the prioritized want; the client now needs to take a look at how achieving their want will improve their lives.

The **Output** of this segment is a the filtered topic resulting in less pain and more joy; the client now knows what they want...and why.

SEGMENT 2: MOTIVATION
Training & Discussion

1. **Purpose of the Segment**

   a. The purpose of this segment is to filter the desired want to determine that the achievement of that want will result in either less pain or more joy. Through conversation about rewards, benefits, consequences and associated feelings, the client will better understand what drives their desire for change.

   b. Typically the client wants to change for one of two reasons: (1) seeking pleasure, (2) avoiding pain. An example of seeking pleasure: I want this promotion because I will be able to afford a bigger house for my family. An example of avoiding pain: If I don't minimize my stress at work I will have a heart attack.

   c. Sometimes, through the process of reviewing the motivation of the want, the client will wish to change or refine what they want. For example: I guess having more money to do things with my wife would be nice (shallow want) but what I really want is for our relationship to improve and us to feel closer (deeper want).

2. **Input**

   a. The input is a prioritized want (which is the same as the output from the *WANT* segment).

   b. The topic should be clear, attainable, relevant to the client, and within their control. It needs to be cleanly stated by the client and not assumed as important by the coach.

3. Output

a. The output of this segment is a filtered topic resulting in less pain or more joy. This means that the client has selected a topic of discussion and has evaluated the topic in terms of the rewards, consequences, and benefits.

4. Guides

a. Guides in the *MOTIVATION* segment, are the boxes labeled Rewards, Consequences, Benefits, Feeling Filter, Joy, and Pain.

b. The coach will guide the client through identifying the Rewards, Consequences, or Benefits. Answers from these questions are often superficial and need to be run through the Feelings Filter to illustrate the most powerful sources of motivation for the client. Then, the client identifies whether their want can move them toward reducing their pain or achieving greater joy.

5. Definitions

a. Motivation: Motivation is the internal force that engages and sustains us in achieving change.

b. Rewards: A reward is the return on investment for achieving new behaviors.

c. Benefits: A benefit is something that promotes or enhances well-being.

d. Consequences: Consequences are the expected result or outcome if a goal or want is achieved. Consequences are frequently considered negative; however, it's important to know that consequences are neutral... they are what they are.

e.   Feeling filter: The feeling filter is a series of questions which explore the rewards, benefits and consequences of a potential action and are used to get at the underlying emotions driving a particular want.

f.   Joy: Joy is the ongoing pursuit of a worthwhile goal.

g.   Pain: Pain can be physical discomfort. Pain can also be the realization by the client that actions are being taken, either by the client or others, which are not consistent with the client's values and beliefs. It's important to know that this pain can be more spiritual and emotional in nature rather than physical pain.

h.   Filtered topic: The filtered topic is a want selected by the client for continued discussion.

6.   **Questions**

SUPPORT LEADING

Q-tip #1:   Why important?

Expanded question #1: So, why is getting/doing/being this want or topic so important?

Discussion #1: This question is used to start the inquiry into the motives behind the want. It is a broad question and should be repeated to get down to the basic emotions. Early responses are usually intellectual or superficial and the coach needs to cause the client to explore more deeply.

Q-tip #2:   What are the benefits?

Expanded question #2: What are the rewards and benefits that you would gain if you achieve your want?

Discussion #2: This is a good early question or follow up question to why this want is important. This question is also useful to get the client to look at the gain or positive side of the want. Sometimes clients focus on the negative side and the coach should try to elicit both positive and negative perspectives of the want. This helps the client refocus on the possibilities of achieving less pain or more joy.

Q-tip #3:   Why want more?

Expanded question #3: Why do you want more of that...what will that do for you?

Discussion #3: This question is used as an additional question to help the client go deeper into the payoffs. The goal of the coach, at this point, is to help the client go beyond superficial to a deeper, emotional point of view.

OBSTACLE LEADING

Q-tip #4:   Why want less?

Expanded question #4: Why would you want less of that (the prioritized item proposed by client)?

Discussion #4: Sometimes the client shows signs of being overwhelmed or their minds are unfocused. Use this question when a client says they want less of....something. Ask *why* in order to help the client dig deeper expose the emotional need behind the want.

Q-tip #5:   Consequence of no change?

Expanded question #5: What would be the consequence if things don't change, how would you be affected?

Discussion #5: This is a good question to get at obvious or superficial reasons for a want. It can also be used if a client is stuck, freeing the client to make an emotional connection with their perceptions of the topic. This question is best used after a benefits inquiry. Clients often are in a state of toleration when they have a long time or reoccurring problem or complaint. In that place they often think about what they want but may ignore what the problem is costing them. Use this question to deeply explore the consequences. This strategy can often provide more incentive for change than focusing on the positive. Some people are more motivated by consequence avoidance than reward or gain.

Q-tip #6:   Is there anything else?

Expanded question #6: Is there anything else that this action or want might cost you?

Discussion #6: A good follow up to the exploration of consequence. This line of questioning can surface substantial payoffs. It can cause breakthroughs in such things as suppressed emotions, hidden fears, or confused beliefs.

SUPPORT BRIDGING

Q-tip #7:   What new feelings does this bring up?

Expanded question #7: How would it feel to have achieved your want? What NEW feelings does talking about this bring up?

Discussion #7: This is a good follow up the examination of what would be different. This question can also be used when the client is responding with only obvious or emotionless responses. It is a deeper question that causes the client to think about feelings associated with change. It is often new and sometimes uncomfortable territory for some clients.

Q-tip #8:   Does that bring joy?

Expanded question #8: So, will accomplishing this want bring you joy or happiness? What is joy for you? What is happiness for you? Do you know what joy or happiness is?

Discussion #8: This might be a very hard question for many clients. An explanation of what joy is can reveal a great deal about what motivates a client. The trick, as a coach, is to help the client move from minimizing pain…and moving toward joy. <u>But</u> … the client needs to know (experience) what joy <u>is</u> in order to move toward it.

Q-tip #9: What did you learn from that?

Expanded question #9: Now that you have identified the desired output, what did you learn from that…about yourself, your capabilities? How can you use this new information in the future?

Discussion #9: This is a question which can be asked at the end of each segment. It is important to the client to acknowledge any moment of awareness or achievement…and why that awareness/achievement is important. This will permit the client to transport this new skill of realization to other opportunities throughout the process. The real question is….what did the client learn that is unique to this segment?

OBSTACLE BRIDGING

Question #10:   Anything stopping you?

Expanded question #10: Is there anything that would stop you from moving forward on this goal?

Discussion #10: This is a good double check before moving to the next segment to make sure the coach isn't dragging the client forward. It is also a good feeder question into issues. The client will either address their reservations about the rewards or start right into the *ISSUES* segment.

Q-tip #11:   What if it didn't work?

Expanded question #11: What is the worst that could happen? What do you actually expect? Is failure a real possibility? Could you survive the down side of trying to do this?

Discussion #11: Use this question to get a casual feel for how a client handles failure. (**Coach's Note: This question is not about going** *deeply into the obstacles for this want. That will be explored in greater depth in the segment on FORCE ANALYSIS.*)

It also helps the client explore the risk side of a change effort. Estimating the amount of risk involved prepares the client to better make the decision to start or pass on this want.

Q-tip #12:   Will this reduce your pain?

Expanded question #12: How would it feel if you won, if you got what you wanted to accomplish…if everything worked out for the best? Would that reduce your pain?

Discussion #12: This question is about pain. If the client got what they wanted, truly wanted, would it actually reduce their perceived pain? Does the client have a pattern of perceiving the world negatively…of always being in pain?

SEGMENT 3: ISSUES

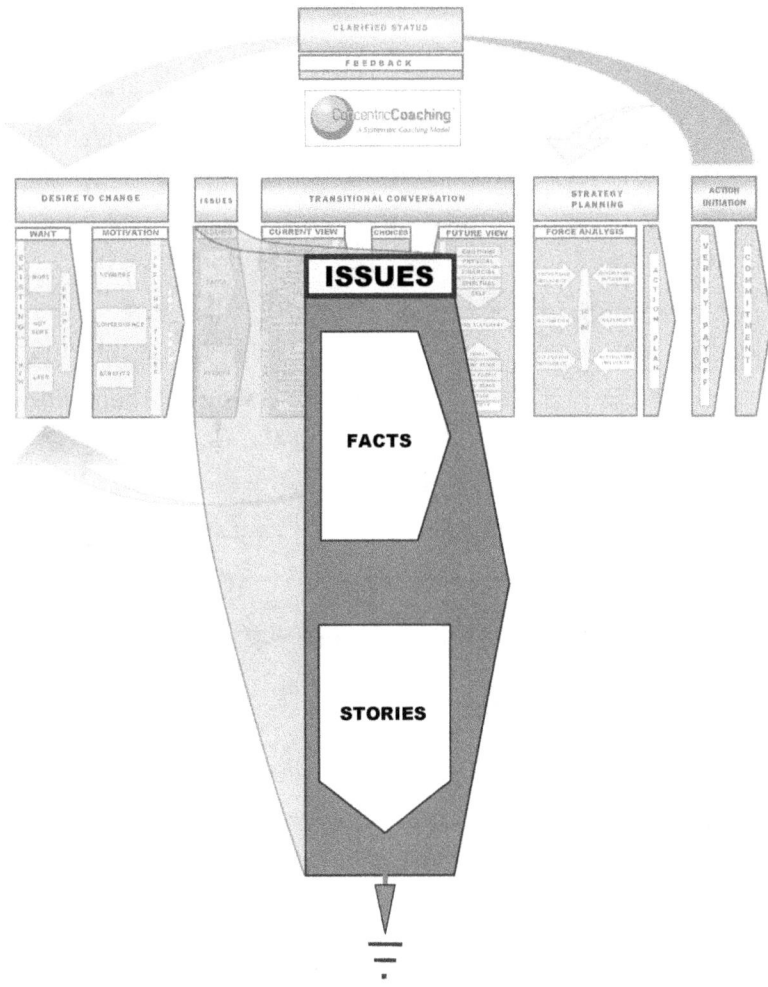

Table of Q-TIP Questions

Support Leading	Support Bridging
1. What can you tell me? 2. How does that contribute? 3. Do you know what a "story" is?	7. What else is important to know? 8. Is that true? 9. What did you learn from that?
Input *Filtered topic resulting in less pain & more joy* ⇨	**Output** *Story-free, relevant facts about topic* ⇨
4. Is that a story? 5. Are we getting off topic? 6. Need to vent?	10. What does that story contribute? 11. Is that relevant information? 12. How would others view that info?
Obstacle Leading	**Obstacle Bridging**

Intention of the Q-TIPs for this segment:

This segment is all about pulling together the facts about the client's want.

The **Input** is the filtered topic resulting in less pain and more joy; now the client needs to convert the topic into a topic with the facts and issues on the table.

The **Output** of this segment are the story –free, relevant facts about the topic; this step clears the way for the client to move toward their want.

SEGMENT 3: ISSUES
Training & Discussion

1. **Purpose of the Segment**

   a. The purpose of this segment is to provide the client with a framework within which to narrow the scope of what they want.

   b. Specifically, we need to get more facts. We need to refine our understanding of what the client REALLY wants and why. Additionally, this is where stories are acknowledged and, possibly removed, from the conversation.

2. **Input**

   a. The input to this segment, as is generally the case, is the output from the previous segment. The previous segment was *MOTIVATION* and the output from that segment was Filtered topic resulting in less pain or more joy. Therefore, the input to this segment is the same – Filtered topic resulting in less pain or more joy.

   b. It is important to have the topic clearly specified by the client. It is the foundation of the rest of the client's progress.

   c. The issue of less pain and more gain is, at this point, more for the coach than the client. The point of this input is that it is important for the coach to notice the trend of the client – is the client striving to move away from something they don't want or toward what they do want? One of the many values that a coach can add to the coaching process is to influence the client toward a more positive approach to behavior change and beliefs rather than just situation avoidance.

3. Output

a. The output of the *ISSUES* segment is the story free, relevant facts about the topic.

b. When a client is having difficulty discussing the root cause of a problem the client may attempt to tell a story in order to have you better understand or sympathize with the client's situation. Telling a brief story one time can be very productive in understanding the client's perspective on a particular situation. On the other hand, repeating the story in defense of not changing is another issue. It is important for the coach to short circuit or stop the story telling as quickly as possible.

c. Additionally, it is important for both the client and the coach to identify all available facts about the topic. These facts help define the framework for the development and identification of the beliefs held by the client about the subject.

d. Facts include information about external environments, internal environments, beliefs, data or anything else relevant to the discussion.

e. It should be noted that this segment is designed to be moved through relatively quickly.

4. Guides

a. The guides for the *ISSUES* segment are facts and stories.

b. The facts guide is designed to keep the coach on track, to look for facts and relevant data about the selected topic. Facts might include information about attitudes, aptitudes, resources, strategies, or other people and places.

c. The stories guide is one of the most important symbols within the model. If you are familiar with any electrical diagrams, you may recognize the arrow and triple lines. This is the diagram symbol for a short circuit. The analogy here is that when a client continues to use stories or tells a long winded story, it is important to manage the process and stop the story as quickly as possible. In some cases, it's a valuable technique to bring the story telling up as an issue in and of itself.

5. Definitions:

a. Facts: Facts, in the context of coaching, are beliefs, strongly held opinions, and other data which define the issue for the client. It is important for the coach to realize that facts aren't always true...they are just believed to be true. Part of the coaching process is the determination if facts are true.

b. Stories: Stories are the natural defense of the client. A story is a narrative description of an occurrence, a situation, or an analogy answering a question posed by the coach. Often the client will weave a story around themselves to protect against uncomfortable questions, the possibility of change, or sometimes it's just the way the client expresses themselves. It is important to keep the stories to a minimum...and repeating stories to an absolute minimum. It is a handy trick to have a routine phrase or question to use when trying to short circuit a client out of a story.

c. Story-free: Story-free means that the client has identified and faced the facts of the particular situation. It's not that a story hasn't been told, it's more that the story is brief, in context, relevant, and makes a point – ONCE!!

d. Relevant: The word relevant in terms of coaching means that the information provided by the client pertains to the subject at hand. That the data provided is useful to the client. And most importantly, that the information is factual. Beliefs will be evaluated in another segment, but for facts to have any bearing on the issue at hand, they must be relevant to the conversation. Similar to stories, clients may sometimes present information which might even be true...but has no relevance to the subject being discussed.

e. Short circuit: Short circuit is an electrical term meaning to divert or stop a current in an electrical circuit. In a coaching sense, what is meant by that in the conversation...the repetitive story....is stopped. The story needs to be brief, relevant, and ONCE!! After that, it's just a defense mechanism. This should obviously be done with appropriate tact. It is important, however, to let the client know that they are storytelling, not just rudely interrupt the client.

6. **Questions**

SUPPORT LEADING

Q-tip #1:   What can you tell me?

Expanded question #1: What can you tell me about that topic? Or, why don't you already have your want?

Discussion #1: This is a good first question after clearly identifying the motives necessary to change. It starts the client discussing the issues associated with the want. The alternative question "Why don't you already have your want?" can be a little more confrontational if not said carefully. But it allows for all the stories that can be holding a client back. Stories can tell the coach a lot about the client.

Q-tip #2:   How does that contribute?

Expanded question #2: So, how does what you just said contribute to the selected topic?

Discussion #2: Use this question when the client is rambling or talking about things that don't seem pertinent to the topic.

Q-tip #3:   Do you know what a story is?

Expanded question #3: Do you know what a story is?

Discussion #3: This is a question asked from a place of curiosity; if the client is a story teller it is important that the client understand what a story is…how it relates to a topic/goal…and how a story can be both supportive and obstructive to the change process. Supportive in the sense that sometimes the facts need to be placed in context; obstructive in the sense that the story should not be used as a defense against getting to the point and clouding the truth. For example: "My boss is a jerk". Although the problem is probably very obvious to the client, this statement needs clarification. "Jerk" is a story and may cloud the truth. The truth may be that the boss is a jerk; or the truth may be that the employee isn't following job rules; the boss is having personal problems, etc. The coach needs to clarify attitudes that allowed the client to create the story "jerk". This is also a great place (during the story telling) for the coach to observe potential key statements containing words such as: should….would….could have….much pain…..great joy….happens repeatedly….always…never…etc.

OBSTACLE LEADING

Q-tip #4:   Is that a story?

Expanded question #4: I've heard what you're saying, but are you telling (or softer: expressing) a story or contributing to the facts of the topic?

Discussion #4: This is a short circuit question. Use it when a client seems to be sharing opinions or using generalities that don't contribute to the issue at hand. It is important to get permission from the client to move off a story…even if you have to ask firmly.

Q-tip #5:   Are we getting off topic?

Expanded question #5: Are we getting off the topic? Is this something that is contributing to the topic at hand?

Discussion #5: This question is used when the client keeps changing topics. It can be a shift in the response as the client is speaking or a response that has nothing to do with the question. By putting this question to the client you are looking to them to reveal the reason for this diversion.

Q-tip #6:   Need to vent?

Expanded question #6: Is there something that you need to just talk about/vent ...or is this something we need to address? Is there anything else? This sounds like something you really needed to say....? It feels like there is a lot of emotion behind what you're saying...do you need to vent?

Discussion #6:   Venting is the expression of a story driven by high emotion. Is the client actually venting or just complaining? Once the coach determines that the client is venting, acknowledge the venting, and purposefully give permission to the client to (briefly) vent. When the client finishes venting, acknowledge the client's frustration, and then ask the client how that information might be used to move the issue forward.

SUPPORT BRIDGING

Q-tip #7:   What else is important to know?

Expanded question #7: What else about that is important to know?

Discussion #7: Use this question to keep the data coming. There are almost always things unsaid and this question helps the client dig deeper.

Q-tip #8:   Is that true?

Expanded question #8: How do you know that's true? Is what you just said actually true or is that what you believe to be true? What makes you think it's true....what's your evidence? How would you confirm that information if you weren't absolutely assured it was true? (Said supportively...rather than assertively)

Discussion #8: When a client states something that doesn't sound accurate or sounds like an opinion, the coach needs to dig deeper. It's important to move the client from opinion to evidence; from evidence to fact.

Q-tip #9: What did you learn from that?

Expanded question #9: Now that you have identified the desired output, what did you learn from that...about yourself, your capabilities? How can you use this new information in the future?

Discussion #9: This is a question which can be asked at the end of each segment. It is important to the client to acknowledge any moment of awareness or achievement...and why that awareness/achievement is important. This will permit the client to transport this new skill of realization to other opportunities throughout the process. The real question is....what did the client learn that is unique to this segment?

OBSTACLE BRIDGING

Q-tip #10: What does that story contribute?

Expanded question #10: Can you tell me how that story contributes to what we are talking about? (Said without judgment)

Discussion #10: When the client keeps referencing a story, this question is useful to disrupt the pattern. If the client says the story doesn't contribute, you can also ask if there is a personal payoff to using the story. The goal here is to help the client dissolve the story, and the frequent retelling of a story, that is getting in the way of the facts.

Q-tip #11: Is that relevant information?

Expanded question #11: Does that information contribute to what we are talking about....how should we use that information?

Discussion #11: Use this question when information being provided by the client doesn't <u>seem</u> relevant. By asking this question we can get additional information that helps the coach understand the relevance expressed by the client. At the same time, what the client is sharing may NOT be relevant in which case; the coach needs to get the client back on track.

Q-tip #12:   How would others view that information?

Expanded question #12: How would others view that information? Who would have a different slant or perspective…and what would that alternate perspective be?

Discussion #12: Alternative perspectives can raise challenges to the client's beliefs. This question helps the client view their opinion through the eyes of another person. Even if the client believes the information to be true doesn't necessarily make it true.

SEGMENT 4: CURRENT VIEW

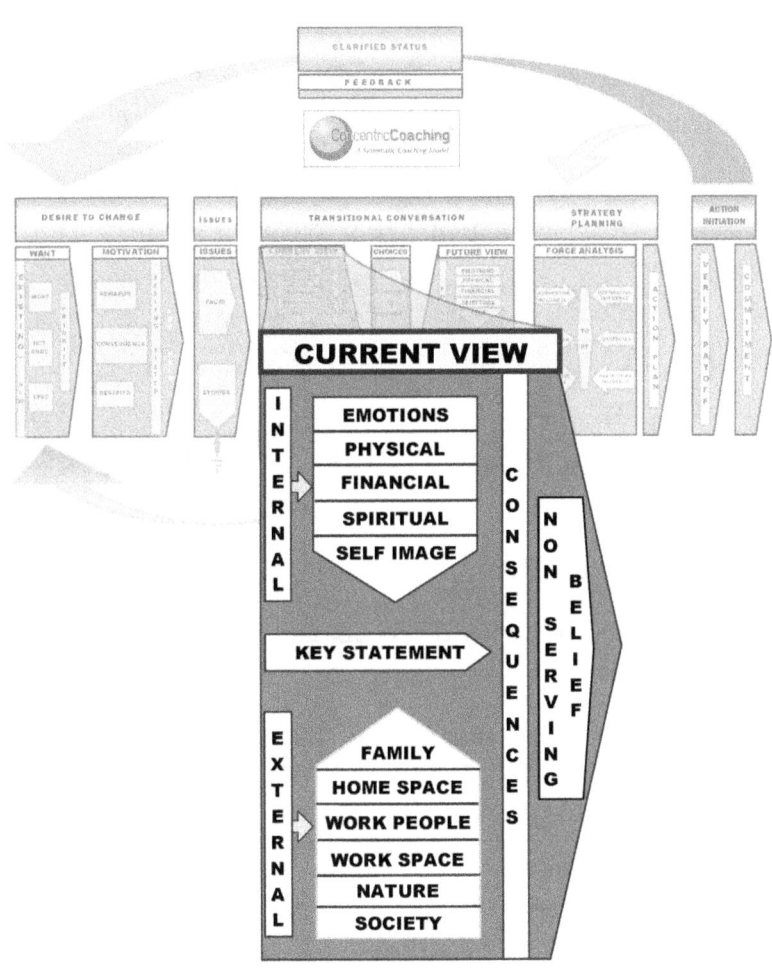

Table of Q-TIP Questions

Support Leading	Support Bridging
1. Tell me more about that? 2. Is that in your control? 3. What do you mean by.....?	7. What will happen if....? 8. Why do you believe that? 9. What did you learn from that?
Input Story-free, relevant facts about topic ⇨	**Output** Filtered key statements defining non-serving beliefs ⇨
4. What if NOT in control of that? 5. Who DOES control that? 6. Is that what you're saying?	10. How's that working for you? 11. Scan of your environments? 12. Is that who you are/want to be?
Obstacle Leading	**Obstacle Bridging**

Intention of the Q-TIPs for this segment:

This segment is all about identifying beliefs that the client has that may not be serving them well.

The **Input** is the story –free, relevant facts about the topic; now the client needs to explore their want to separate what is working from what is not working.

The **Output** of this segment is a filtered key statement defining not serving beliefs; the important point here is the specification of the key statement and acknowledgement of the non-serving beliefs.

SEGMENT 4: CURRENT VIEW
Training & Discussion

I. **Purpose of the Segment**

    a.   The purpose of this segment is to work with the client to arrive at a key statement filtered through the client's beliefs.

    b.   The identification of a key statement is critical in beginning the exploration of the depth necessary to find the obstacles to moving the client forward. You can think of the key statement as the "ah ha" phrase that the client says which triggers you to what is really happening in the client's mind. Frequently the statement will be said under their breath or in passing or as part of a transition to another part of a conversation. Buried within in key statement is the root of where the client is.

2. **Input**

    a.   The input to this segment, as is generally the case, is the output from the previous segment. The previous segment is *ISSUES* and the output from that segment is Story free, relevant facts about the topic; therefore, the input to this segment is the same.

    b.   The trick is to get the client to clearly specify precisely what <u>they</u> want to work on. It makes the client feel like they have a path for the coaching session...and the coach has a solid, concrete place to start.

    c.   The truth of the matter is that frequently the session might take another turn...but at least there is an existing preliminary goal.

3. Output

a. The output of the *CURRENT VIEW* segment is the Filtered key statements defining beliefs.

b. This means that the client has shared with the coach a key observation about what they believe and what is important to them...either a viewpoint, a belief, a perspective...something to give you a glimpse of what is really going on in their mind.

c. The key statement needs to be processed through the environments provided in the guides.

d. The environments are split into two groups; internal and external environments. Each of the environments will be more fully described in the guides section to follow.

e. As the discussion with the client progresses, it will become apparent if the concern of the client is one of internal or external environments. Once the client indicates whether the environment is internal or external, the coach has the opportunity to reorient the questions. The reorientation (and refocusing) by the coach will permit the questions to dig deeper into the truth of the problem/opportunity. You may notice as you become more experienced with the environments that, although a client may begin moving through the external environments, they will inevitably return to the internal environments. This is because even if the problem is with someone else/something else the problem will always return back to the perceptions of the client...and back into the internal environments.

f. As the discussion continues, the client will reveal their beliefs about the issue at hand. As the coach moves the client deeper, examining more and more closely the held beliefs, key statements will be exposed. The beliefs and values of the client need to be filtered through the examination of the consequences (both positive and negative) of those beliefs. The beliefs need to be verified (did you hear what was said), validated (what causes you to believe what was said), and challenged (is what was said true...what if it's not?!?) Until finally, the source of the belief is identified, verified, validated and, lastly, acknowledged. This condition is what is referred to as the *CURRENT VIEW*; how things are <u>now</u>.

g.   Then a decision needs to be made regarding the filtered key statement defining the belief....is it a belief the client is going to hold on to (maybe yes, if it's a supportive belief) or change (if making the change will move the client toward their true goal).

4. Guides

a.   This is a complex segment. The *CURRENT VIEW* is meant to provide an opportunity for the client to assess their beliefs and consequences in terms of their internal and external environments. This contrast is triggered by what is called a "key statement".

b.   The key statement is a momentary glimpse into the attitudes and beliefs of the client. Sometimes the statement is made in haste, under their breath, or even as a defensive position. Either way, it is the signal to the coach that a belief is being presented. When a belief is presented, it will then be processed through an environment for validation on it's way to becoming a decision.

c.   The framework for the decision is to examine the beliefs of the client in terms of a set of internal or external environments.

d.   The internal environments look at what makes up the client; their emotions, their perspective on their physical selves, how their finances are, the position on their spirituality, and most importantly, the client's self image. The significant aspect of the internal environments is that it is the environment which is under the direct control of the client.

e. The external environments look at what surrounds the client; their family and spouse, their home space, work people, work spaces, nature, and society in general. The significant aspect of the external environments is that it requires the interaction with others...and is typically NOT within the control of the client.

f. As the key statement is processed through the internal or external environments, the beliefs and attitudes of the client become more clear. The question then becomes "Are these values, beliefs, attitudes, etc. serving the client?" As the key statement is tuned and validated, it needs to be run through the filter of the consequence of accepting or rejecting the particular belief. As the consequences of performance or non-performance are processed, the decision moves closer and closer to what is the source of the non-serving belief.

g. Once the non-serving belief or attitude is specified from the key statement, a decision becomes necessary.....do I (as the client) accept this belief? Or do I choose to make a change!?!

h. It should be noted that the client may be very *full* of information at this point. There is a lot of information to be juggling and processing. Support the client....keep him/her moving forward...and a valuable insight will come of the analysis.

5. Definitions

a. Transitional Conversation: The Transitional Conversation is the building block which compares the as-is, current view to the could-be, future view...as chosen by the client. It is in this building block in which the client's environments are examined, key and action statements are expressed, and choices are made.

b. CURRENT VIEW: The *CURRENT VIEW* is the as-is position of the client on a particular key statement. During this segment, the client will typically conduct an environment scan (enviro-scan), during which a key statement will be expressed. The key statement is the pivotal point to this segment. The key statement is then examined in order to determine the prioritized non-serving beliefs.

c. Key Statement: The key statement is a self-revealing glimpse into the non-serving beliefs, attitudes and values of the client. It is a nearly inadvertent expression of the truth.

d. Internal Environments (IE): The internal environments are those characteristics which define the internal aspects of the client. Typically the internal environments are within the control of the client.

e. (Internal Environment =IE) Emotions: The emotions of the client are the ways in which the client illustrates how they feel about a particular situation.

f. (IE) Physical: The physical environment is an illustration of how the client feels about themselves in terms of body image, sexuality, weight, etc. "How do I feel?"

g. (IE) Financial: The financial environment includes the current state and how client feels about money, acquiring wealth, managing wealth, how well positioned they are in terms of their financial needs, how they are positioned for retirement or the next significant change in their lives. Also included is their perspective on money within their family, a working spouse, etc.

h. (IE) Spiritual: This environment addresses the client's perspective on spirituality to themselves, how the client feels about an external power, something greater than themselves, or support that might be drawn from such a power.

i. (IE) Self Image: The self image environment is all about how the client feels about themselves in a general way. Am I a good person, do I do things well, am I a planner, how do I perceive the views of others, how do I communicate. The self image environment differs from the physical environment in that the self image is the basis for self esteem and personal power.

j. External Environments (EE): The external environments are all about the people, places or things surrounding the client...helping them or hindering them....or both. The internal environments are frequently under the control of the client; the external environments are typically NOT able to be controlled. Managed, maybe.....controlled, almost never.

k. (EE) Family: This environment is a measure of how the client perceives family, spouse, significant others, children, parents, etc. as supporting or inhibiting their actions.

l. (EE) Home Space: The home space environment examines how the client perceives their home and property. Is the home a drain on their energy or a refuge from the stresses of every day life?

m. (EE) Work People: The work people environment examines how the client perceives work associates in a 360° perspective; to include, superiors, peers, subordinates, suppliers, anyone that they might come in contact with in a work related experience.

n. (EE) Work Space: Work space as an environment has taken on an entirely new role as more and more people become self employed. Work space includes where you work, if you work remotely, as well as home space which is dedicated to be used as work. The work space environment also includes any equipment, technology, and instruments which might be used in connection with work.

o. (EE) Nature: The nature environment illustrates how the client perceives the space not captured in home or work environments. This environment would encompass everything from someone else's work space, other people's property, the responsibility acknowledged by the client for the care of nature....anything that is other to the client than that which is theirs.

p. (EE) Society: The societal environment encompasses both everyone outside your inner circle of family and close friends...but it also includes you. Specifically, how you interact with community and others as well as how they interact with you. Is it important to you how you are perceived by others and how you perceive them?

q. Consequences: Consequence is the feedback you receive from the implementation of any behavior. The feedback may be visual (a facial expression), auditory (someone thanking your for helping them), it may be a thing (increased profit from a good business decision) or it may be spiritual (a feeling of peace and calmness from doing something well).

r. Non-Serving Belief: A non-serving belief is an opinion or judgment a client has about themselves and their environments. This opinion may be true...or not. A non-serving belief differs from a supporting belief in that it is not contributing to the positive growth of the client.

s. Environmental Scan (enviro-scan): This scan involves the process of exploring internal and external environments and their respective individual environments. The intent is to have the client routinely scan their environments in order to quickly take stock of where they are with respect to those internal and external influences and beliefs.

6. **Questions**

SUPPORT LEADING

Q-tip #1: Tell me more about that?

Expanded question #1: Can you/would you tell me more about that?

Discussion #1: This segment is where the coach needs to start digging deeper, to convert the facts identified in the previous segment into the feelings, the emotions which enrich the topic. Additionally, the coach is searching for the key statement which is the true point of this segment. The key statement can then be filtered through the environments in order to reach the true desire/need of the client.

Q-tip #2:   Is that in your control?

Expanded question #2: You've been telling me about a situation, is that situation actually in your control? If not, then who/what has the most control?

Discussion #2: These questions are posed in order to figure out which set of environments best address the desire/need of the client. The nexus of control is the measure of the extent to which the client feels in control. The closer the nexus is to the center of the client, the more in control the client would feel. As the nexus of control moves away from the client, the more the client feels that someone/thing else is controlling the situation. This question is attempting to determine where the nexus of control is for the client.

Q-tip #3:   What do you mean by...?

Expanded question #3: What do you mean by that particular emotion/statement .....?

Discussion #3: This question is about exploring the emotions and beliefs of the client. Again, the coach is attempting to more fully examine the beliefs and values of the client while scanning their environments. The important skill for the coach at this point is to listen very carefully. The coach needs to be listening for the key statement in order to identify what the client truly desires or wants to change. (**Coach's Note: This implies that what the client is asking for may be different than what they actually want.**)

Q-tip #4: What if NOT in control of that?

Expanded question #4: What would be the outcome if you weren't in control of that situation?

Discussion #4: This question is the reverse of the control question and has at least two aspects for the client. The first is the obvious question exposing the client to the possibility that he/she might not be in control of the situation. However, there is another more subtle side to this question; what if the client gave up control of the situation. What if the client was desperately holding on to something but needed to let go of it? This question definitely pushes the client into an area where they might not have gone before.

Q-tip #5: Who DOES control that?

Expanded question #5: If you aren't in control of that situation, who is? Is that ok? What is the effect of that other person being in control?

Discussion #5: This question examines the nexus of control in order to determine where the control actually resides. Sometimes the control of a situation is with another person or agency; however, sometimes to the client's surprise, the true control is with themselves.

Q-tip #6: Is that what you're saying?

Expanded question #6: Is "___" what you're saying? Am I hearing that correctly? (This question is not posed in judgment, but to confirm your understanding of what they are trying to say.)

Discussion #6: This question has two functions. The first is a reflective question; verifying with the client what was said. This is a form of clarification. Also, this question can be a verification of the key statement. As mentioned before, a key statement is a reflection of what the client REALLY desires or fears and it's important to verify what was said. Coaches, be careful at this point. Clients may try to disavow what they just said....saying that they may have misspoken; however, more likely, they said what was really on their mind.

SUPPORT BRIDGING

Q-tip #7:   What will happen if...?

Expanded question #7: What would happen if....you didn't do that, you DID do that, you weren't in control, or control wasn't necessary?

Discussion #7: This is another exploratory question. These questions cause the client to dig into their emotions, into their motives, into their beliefs...causing the client to more fully examine how they feel about what they are saying.

Q-tip #8:   Why do you believe that?

Expanded question #8: Why do you believe that? What is the source of that belief? Is that a source of a belief or just a symptom? Is that your opinion or is that a emotional position?

Discussion #8: This is another clarifying question separating emotions from supportable opinions. It should be noted that just because it's an emotion doesn't make it untrue. However, just because the client's statement is firmly made doesn't make it true, either. This question would be asked any time a client makes an emotional, perhaps even key, statement.

Q-tip #9:   What did you learn from that?

Expanded question #9: Now that you have identified the desired output, what did you learn from that...about yourself, your capabilities? How can you use this new information in the future?

Discussion #9: This is a question which can be asked at the end of each segment. It is important to the client to acknowledge any moment of awareness or achievement...and why that awareness/achievement is important. This will permit the client to transport this new skill of realization to other opportunities throughout the process. The real question is….what did the client learn that is unique to this segment?

OBSTACLE BRIDGING

Question #10:   How's that working for you?

Expanded question #10: Is what you are doing TODAY working for you…..is it benefiting you…or are you letting your beliefs get in your way?

Discussion #10: This question can be used very effectively as a stopping question, used to stop the client who might be enthusiastically building a case to do a particular activity. Sometimes the client just needs someone to ask if that behavior or action is actually working for them. Be careful not to let a client launch into a story at this point. Keep the client on track and have them answer the question. Also, watch for a key statement.

Q-tip #11:   Scan of your environments?

Expanded question #11: How does that _____ (environment) affect you?

(Coach's Note: An explanation of an environment scan would be done with the client in this segment to set the stage for a rapid review of the environments at any time.)

Discussion #11: The questions about the environment would include two sets of inquiries: (1) Internal environments and how internal aspects of the client affect the client and (2) External Environments and how external aspects surrounding the client affect the client.

Q-tip #12:   Is that who you are/want to be?

Expanded question #12: (Given a specified belief or set of beliefs on the table) if you did that, would that help you become the person you want to be...or could be? Is that who you are? Does that belief keep you where you are? What beliefs are keeping you where you are?

Discussion #12: This set of questions establishes the source of the non-serving beliefs that the client may have. Once the key statement has been made and the non-serving beliefs challenged, the client will develop a firm sense of the source of their conflict. It is important not to hurry the client through this particular segment. This is a fundamental question and may take some time for the client to come to face what they actually want and can be.

SEGMENT 5: CHOICES

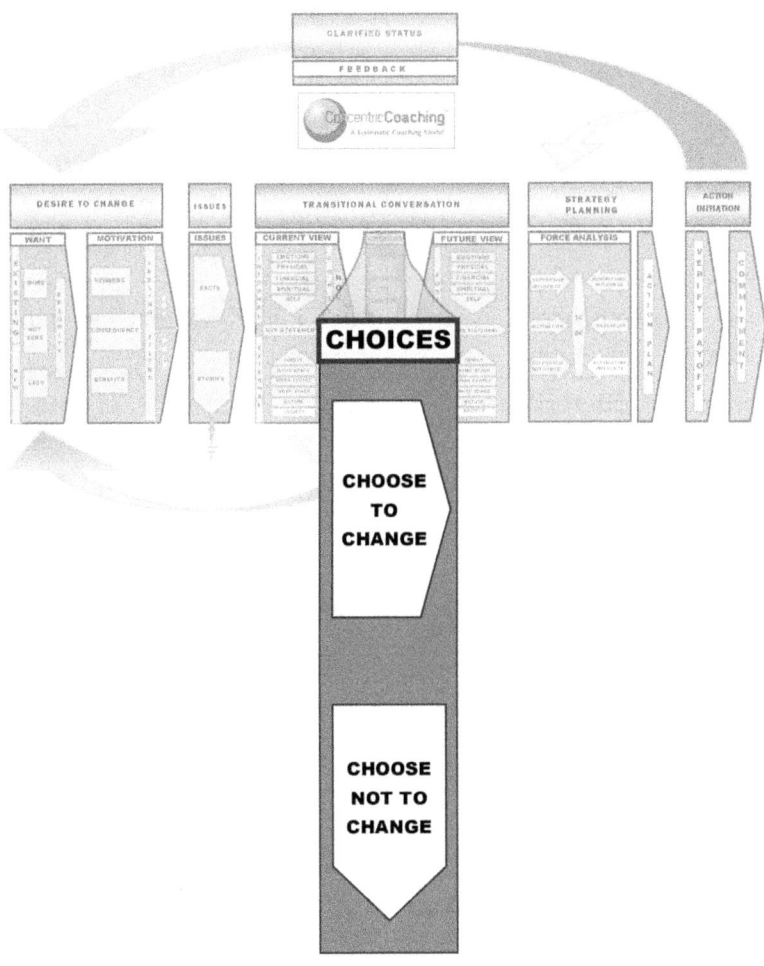

Table of Q-TIP Questions

Support Leading		Support Bridging	
1. Top three (3) non-serving beliefs? 2. What would make a difference? 3. What are you feeling?		7. (Likely) Are you willing to change that..? 8. (Likely) What if change worked? 9. What did you learn from that?	
Input	*Filtered key statements defining non-serving beliefs* ⇨	**Output**	*Choice made to consider change of non-serving belief* ⇨
4. Are you comfortable with change? 5. How do you measure change? 6. Ever been burned with change?		10. (Unlikely) What just happened? 11. (Unlikely) What is cost of not changing? 12. (Unlikely) Good time for a change?	
Obstacle Leading		**Obstacle Bridging**	

Intention of the Q-TIPs for this segment:

This segment is all about choices…and decisions to work on those choices.

The **Input** is filtered key statements defining non-serving beliefs; now is the time for the client to examine which decision is to be made…or even if a decision is appropriate at this time. Perhaps a new want is a better choice.

The **Output** of this segment is a choice made to consider change of non-serving belief; now is the time for the client to decide what to do. Make the choice to change or change what they want.

SEGMENT 5: CHOICES
Training & Discussion

1. Purpose of the Segment

    a.   Choice is all about the client deciding to make a change…or not.

    b.   The function of this segment is to examine the selected topic and determine if this is the right time and opportunity to make the selected change.

    c.   This is a vulnerable time for the client; this is when a client who is feeling unsure may present all sorts of defenses. Equally, the client may uncover additional legitimate obstacles. This is one of two points in the model (the other is the *COMMITMENT* segment) where a clear and concrete statement needs to be made by the client….choose to change…or choose not to change. Either choice is fine…but a decision needs to be made.

2. Input

    a.   The input to this segment is: Filtered key statement defining non-serving beliefs.

    b.   The basis for this segment is the non-serving belief illustrated as a key statement.

    c.   The key statement has been filtered in order to take into account all of the relevant environments which support and obstruct the action desired by the client.

    d.   Now, it's time for the client to make a choice about a non-serving belief.

3. Output

a. The output to this segment is: Choice made to consider change of non-serving belief(s).

b. It is obvious that the point of the *CHOICES* segment is to make a choice. However, you may notice in the output that the choice is being considered rather then immediately undertaken.

c. The reason for this wording is because there are a number of other steps/segments which might cause the client to modify or even reject an accepted choice later on in the process. For example, it might become strategically inappropriate to attend to the change at this time. The change might be too costly. The change might require control by someone else and the client can't make the desired change. It might require someone else's approval to make the change. All of which might be a reason for ultimately NOT choosing to make the change at this time…in this way.

4. Guides

a. The guides within this segment are pretty straightforward; choose to change and choose not to change.

b. The choose-to-change option is selected when the client decides, after exploration and examination, to make the change and continue the process forward.

c. The choose-not-to-change option diverts the client from continuing forward and the model moves the client/coach to two other conditions.

d. The first condition is that the client reconstructs a new key statement consistent with the original concept or desire to change.

e.   The second condition is when the client discards the entire key statement and returns to the *WANT* segment where a completely new want is constructed.

5.   Definitions

a.   Choice: Choice is a concrete decision made by the client to either continue forward with the original want ...OR...the choice is made to not continue forward and revise the want.

b.   Concrete Decision: A concrete decision is a decision, made by the client, which is clear, unambiguous, and actionable. An example of a concrete decision is, when skydiving, to jump out of the plane. (Although a bit dramatic, it makes the point clearly) In this case, it's clear that jumping out of the plane is necessary to go skydiving, it is very clear what the desire of the jumper is, and it is certainly a clear action.

6.   Questions

SUPPORT LEADING

Q-tip #1:   Top three (3) non-serving beliefs?

Expanded question #1: Can you identify your top three (3) non-serving beliefs?

Discussion #1: This where the client will hone in on creating priorities. Sometimes there is just one belief that needs to be considered, other times it's more than one. However, the conversation here is about identifying what is the most important candidate for change to the client.

Q-tip #2:   What would make a difference?

Expanded question #2: If you changed one or all of your identified non-serving beliefs, would that make a difference in your life?

Discussion #2: This is another question that gives the client an opportunity to share discoveries that, if changed, would make a difference in reaching their goal. For example: The client always seemed to believe that to be successful he had to do everything. If that wasn't true and there was a way for others to do more, it would make a big difference in the amount of time he had to work, and the amount of time he could spend with his family. This might be a deciding influence to choose to change.

Q-tip #3:   What are you feeling?

Expanded question #3: How is your body reacting to your new awareness of your non-serving beliefs? How is your body reacting to saying it out loud?

Discussion #3: This question helps the client to get out of their head…to stop intellectualizing…and respond to the feelings their body is experiencing (stress, anxiety, etc.) It clears the path for the client to consider their emotions, which are necessary to allow a full and complete choice.

OBSTACLE LEADING

Q-tip #4:   Are you (un)comfortable with change?

Expanded question #4: Did it turn out that the fear was justified? What's your perspective on making mistakes? Are mistakes permitted/supported in your work/home environment? (**Coach's Note: Pick any appropriate environment.**)

Discussion #4: Sometimes clients deny, resist and fear change. These questions can be used when the coach senses resistance or fear to change. It can also be used to check with clients about self knowledge or past patterns relating to change.

Q-tip #5:   How do you measure change?

Expanded question #5: How do you measure change? How do you know if you are making a true change? How do you know when you are done making the change?

Discussion #5: This question is actually two categories of questions. The first question is a metrics question…how is change measured by the client. The second question responds to the result of that metric….how do you know when you have reached the goal…and how do you know if you don't reach the goal.

(Coach's Note: Make sure the client doesn't obsess about the metric and lose track of the real goal.)

Q-tip #6: **Ever been burned with a change?**

Expanded question #6: Have you ever been burned when making a change? Do you know more today than you did then? Would that inhibit you from MAKING a change today? Would what you know now have stopped you from getting burned then? Do you think that what you know now might minimize getting burned tomorrow (making a change easier/safer)?

Discussion #6: When the client seems reluctant to change in spite of great potential reward, the coach should explore if there have been bad past experiences. This questioning can help the client discover if there is an opportunity to learn something which would prevent them from making the same mistake this time.

SUPPORT BRIDGING

Q-tip #7: **(Likely) Are you willing to change that......?**

Expanded question #7: Is it is likely that you are going to make a change? Which change?

Discussion #7: This is another question to be used when the potential payoff is high but the client is hesitant. Sometimes the client just needs an encouraging nudge. This is an opportunity for the coach to challenge the client; do it!! If not now, when?

Q-tip #8:   (Likely) What if change worked?

Expanded question #8: If it's likely that you will make the attempt to make the change, what if desired change actually worked? What if the change effort was wildly successful? What would it mean about you and to you?

Discussion #8: This is another question designed to help clients overcome hesitancy on their part. It can also highlight good feelings associated with potential rewards and benefits.

Q-tip #9:   What did you learn from that?

Expanded question #9: Now that you have identified the desired output, what did you learn from that...about yourself, your capabilities? How can you use this new information in the future?

Discussion #9: This is a question which can be asked at the end of each segment. It is important to the client to acknowledge any moment of awareness or achievement...and why that awareness/achievement is important. This will permit the client to transport this new skill of realization to other opportunities throughout the process. The real question is....what did the client learn that is unique to this segment?

OBSTACLE BRIDGING

Q-tip #10:   (Unlikely) What just happened?

Expanded question #10: Did something just occur to you that made you suddenly believe that you couldn't change if you wanted to....what just happened? What has changed...changed your mind? You were expressing a belief that didn't seem to be working for you....and you suddenly reversed what seemed like an obvious change? What just happened?

Discussion #10: Use these questions if the client seems to have a sudden shift in energy or direction and is hesitant to want to change.

This is an opportunity for the coach to notice one of two things, (1) a pattern of intellectual agreement, but then hesitancy to take action and/or (2) the client may have identified a new obstacle preventing them from making a decision.

Q-tip #11:　(Unlikely) What is the cost of NOT changing?

Expanded question #11: It sounds like you might not want to change that belief/action/behavior/environment, is that a correct perception? What is the cost to NOT making the proposed change?

Discussion #11: This is a good checking question when a client has chosen not to proceed. It allows the client to explore or review obvious or hidden consequences that might occur with a choice not to change. The goal here is to help the client be assured he/she is making the best decision not to convince him/her to change.

(Coach's Note: This is a time when the client might shift into story telling.)

Q-tip #12:　(Unlikely) Good time for a change?

Expanded question #12: Is this a good time for the change? If not now, when? What would have to be different to start a change?

Discussion #12: Sometimes the decision not to change is just a timing issue. This question should be asked to clarify if the want has value, should it be saved for a later date, and if so, when.

SEGMENT 6: FUTURE VIEW

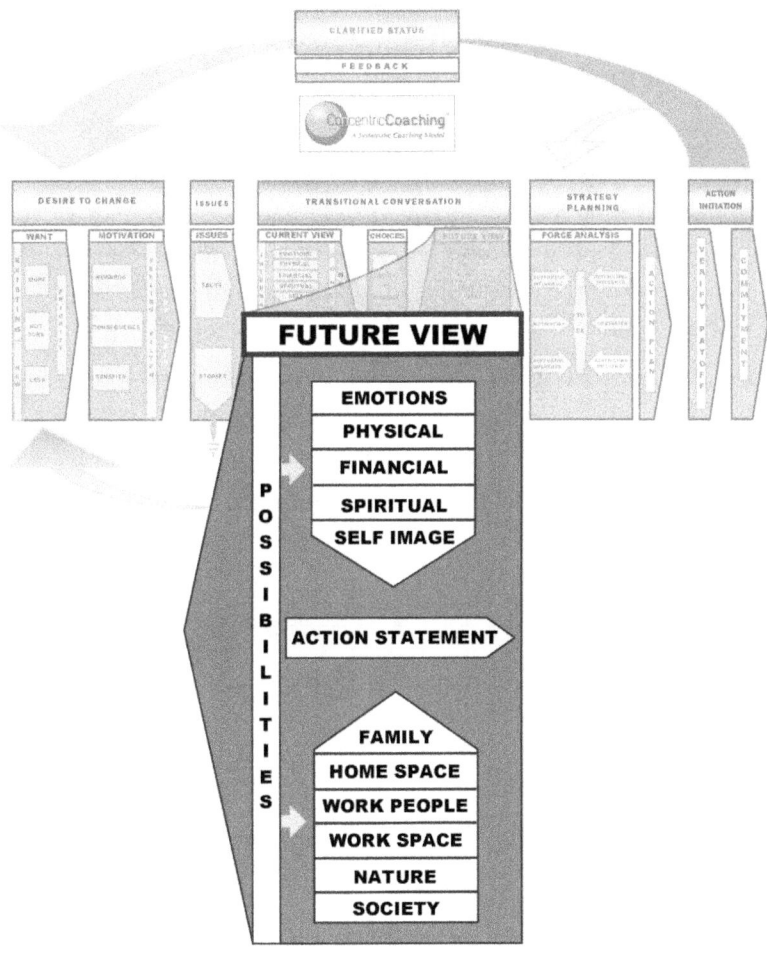

Table of Q-TIP Questions

Support Leading		Support Bridging	
1. What are your priorities? 2. How construct a new belief? 3. How new belief affects environments?		7. How belief move you? 8. What actions would produce want? 9. What did you learn from that?	
Input *Choice made to consider change of non-serving belief*	⇨	**Output** *Potential action statement*	⇨
4. Who might get in the way of new belief? 5. Any hindering habits? 6. Can live with the new change?		10. Which actions aren't comfortable? 11. Your action(s) affect anyone else? 12. How manage if affects someone?	
Obstacle Leading		**Obstacle Bridging**	

Intention of the Q-TIPs for this segment:

This segment is all about not just what is…but what could be.

The **Input** is choice made to consider change of non-serving belief; this is the engine for constructing a new view of what can be accomplished.

The **Output** of this segment is a potential action statement; this is the action statement that is being considered for development of an action plan.

SEGMENT 6: FUTURE VIEW
Training & Discussion

1. **Purpose of the Segment**

   a. The purpose of the *FUTURE VIEW* segment is to convert a processed key statement or non-serving belief into a potential action statement.

   b. It should be noted that the *FUTURE VIEW* is a mirror image of the *CURRENT VIEW*. This is for a reason. In the *CURRENT VIEW* segment the client expresses a belief and the belief is challenged and processed as non-serving. If a change is identified and necessary (and the client chooses to make the change), then in this segment the process is reversed....leading from the source of the belief, the possibilities are examined, beliefs are reevaluated and supportive and obstacle environments are considered ...resulting in a potentially new action statement.

   c. Therefore, this segment converts the old non-serving belief into a new supporting belief and develops the subsequent action necessary to permit and support the new belief.

   d. It is important to have the client leave this segment confident in the possibilities, in their decision making ability, and confident in their potential actions.

2. **Input**

   a. The input to the *FUTURE VIEW* segment is a choice made to consider a change of non-serving belief(s).

   b. The belief must be clear, specified, achievable and most importantly, acknowledged by the client as something that the client wants to change.

c. It is important, at this stage, that the client fully own the belief that is to change. If the belief is a result of the coaches influence or the coaches agenda….the client is less likely to actually follow through on the change to the identified belief.

3. Output

a. The output of the *FUTURE VIEW* segment is a potential action statement.

b. The potential action statement is only that….a <u>potential</u> action statement. The reason why the statement is considered as a potential action statement is because the client has yet to consider all of the potential supportive and restricting influences of the change.

4. Guides

a. The guides in the *FUTURE VIEW* segment are nearly identical to those in the *CURRENT VIEW* and only the differences will be described here.

b. The possibilities guide is where the coach explores all of the possibilities of the potential action with the client. Possibilities include the examination of alternative beliefs. This does NOT imply that the coach has to come up with all of the alternatives; however, this is an excellent opportunity to strategically engage the client to consider newer, larger ways of looking at a situation.

c. Similar to the *CURRENT VIEW* environments, the *FUTURE VIEW* environments are the same. Similarly, an enviro-scan done here is exactly the same as before. The only difference in this segment is that the client is looking forward to what <u>could be</u> rather than a historical view of <u>what is/was</u>.

d.   The action statement is declaration by the client of the specific action they want to take. Similar to the key statement in the previous segment, the action statement is the expression of what the client really would like to do. Help the client be clear about what action they would really like to take. Listen carefully!!

5. Definitions

a.   Possibilities: The possibilities guide is the step where the client examines the possibilities that are presented when considering a new belief; both supportive and obstructive.

There is another aspect of possibilities that needs to be examined. This segment provides an opportunity for a larger view...a stretch goal... by the client. This means that, when the client (and the coach) arrive at the best three candidate actions, the coach might encourage a radical expansion of their current view. This is where the coach earns their pay...this is where the coach help the client stretch toward their maximum potential. This is all about moving the client out of their comfort zone (maybe the coach's comfort zone) to a place where there is true growth.

b.   Supporting Beliefs: The supporting beliefs are candidate beliefs which are on the table...and still need to be run through an environment scan to determine if the candidate supporting belief, and subsequent actions, leads the client ultimately to their indicated want.

c.   Action Statement: The action statement is the specified, actionable, observable change in belief proposed by the client for consideration to change. It is a declarative statement of intent.

6.   Questions

SUPPORT LEADING

Q-tip #1:   What are your priorities?

Expanded question #1: Can you prioritize your non-serving beliefs; if more than one?

Discussion #1: In this case, the coach is causing the client to concretely state their non-serving beliefs. Then the client is asked to prioritize those beliefs in order to construct new beliefs.

Q-tip #2:   How construct a new belief?

Expanded question #2: Given a non-serving belief, how might you construct a new supporting belief? What if there were no restrictions, nothing to stop you from achieving ANYTHING? What would it look like? Go nuts...what COULD you do? What is your GREATEST possibility?

Discussion #2: Having prioritized the non-serving beliefs, the client now needs to start assembling prospective (future view) beliefs. The client needs to state the belief in a supportive and challenging way.

(Coach's Note: This question is about moving the client to a place of maximum potential...WAY outside their comfort zone...and maybe yours? This could lead to the big payoff for the client.)

Q-tip #3:   How new belief affects environments?

Expanded question #3: Can you describe how that new supporting belief will affect your internal and external environments (Enviro-Scan)?

Discussion #3: Once the candidate belief has been identified, the client needs to conduct an environment scan to check how that belief will impact both internal and external environments. In the *CURRENT VIEW* segment, the intent was to see how the environments affected the belief; here we're trying to check how the new belief affects the environments.

Q-tip #4:   Who might get in the way of new belief?
Expanded question #4: Who might get in the way of your new belief system? Does someone else have to change to permit your belief to work?

Discussion #4: Any change that the client makes affects everyone around him/her. The question here is identifying <u>who</u> is being affected and in what way. Then, the client needs to account for anyone who might not be supportive of their supporting belief.

Q-tip #5:   Any hindering habits?

Expanded question #5: Are there any old/hindering habits that you have that might get in your way?

Discussion #5: This question is designed to help the client identify any old or hindering habits which might be an obstacle to the new belief. Habits which once worked might now present an obstacle.

Q-tip #6:   Can live with the new change?

Expanded question #6: Can you live with the new change? Why can't you tolerate the change? (Asked without judgment…pure curiosity) What is causing the push back?

Discussion #6: Just because a new belief sounds good doesn't mean the new belief will fit into the life of the client. What is it about the change that the client is pushing back against? Is the resistance based in fear, a lack of information, a lack of confidence, a challenge to their spirituality…..or any number of other environmental issues?

SUPPORT BRIDGING

Q-tip #7:   How belief move you?

Expanded question #7: How might the candidate supporting belief move you to/toward your original want?

Discussion #7: The coach needs to keep the original want in mind.....it's all about the client's agenda. The question here is....will changing the identified belief (non-supporting)...truly move the client toward that want? As the conversation continues to focus on the outcome, an awareness begins to occur as to what the client needs to do to make the want happen.

Q-tip #8:   What actions would produce want?

Expanded question #8: What actions would be necessary to produce the desired want?

Discussion #8: In the previous questions, the client identified the non-serving belief, the future view of the new supporting belief was expressed, now this question is all about converting the candidate supporting belief into a possible action(s). The coach needs to work with the client to clarify all possibilities during the inquiry process.

Q-tip #9:   What did you learn from that?

Expanded question #9: Now that you have identified the desired output, what did you learn from that...about yourself, your capabilities? How can you use this new information in the future?

Discussion #9: This is a question which can be asked at the end of each segment. It is important to the client to acknowledge any moment of awareness or achievement...and why that awareness/achievement is important. This will permit the client to transport this new skill of realization to other opportunities throughout the process. The real question is....what did the client learn that is unique to this segment?

OBSTACLE BRIDGING

Q-tip #10:   Which actions aren't comfortable?

Expanded question #10: Of the actions that you've identified, with which actions aren't you comfortable?

Discussion #10: This question is designed to identify actions which might obstruct performance because of the client being uncomfortable. The associated emotions are not often immediately apparent to the client. This question is all about awareness. This awareness will allow the client to take responsibility for their actions and make the appropriate choices.

Q-tip #11: Your action(s) affect anyone else?

Expanded question #11: Your actions can often affect others; will these actions affect anyone else?

Discussion #11: The coach needs to make sure that the client realizes that they are not isolated…that what they do affects all of their environments. In this particular question, the client needs to examine to what extent their proposed action(s) will affect anyone else around them. This might include family, work, social relationships, etc. Again, this awareness will allow the client to take responsibility for their actions and make the appropriate choices.

Q-tip #12: How manage if affects someone?

Expanded question #12: So, will doing what you want affect anyone else? How will you manage them if what you want to do affects someone else. Do a quick enviro-scan to check for who might be affected.

Discussion #12: This question is NOT about how the client feels about the potential action. It's more about how the client will minimize the negative affects and maximize the positive results with others…following the implementation of the potential action. It's also about anticipating and minimizing barriers that may arise prior to implementation. This question is designed to provide the client with confidence to move forward.

SEGMENT 7: FORCE ANALYSIS

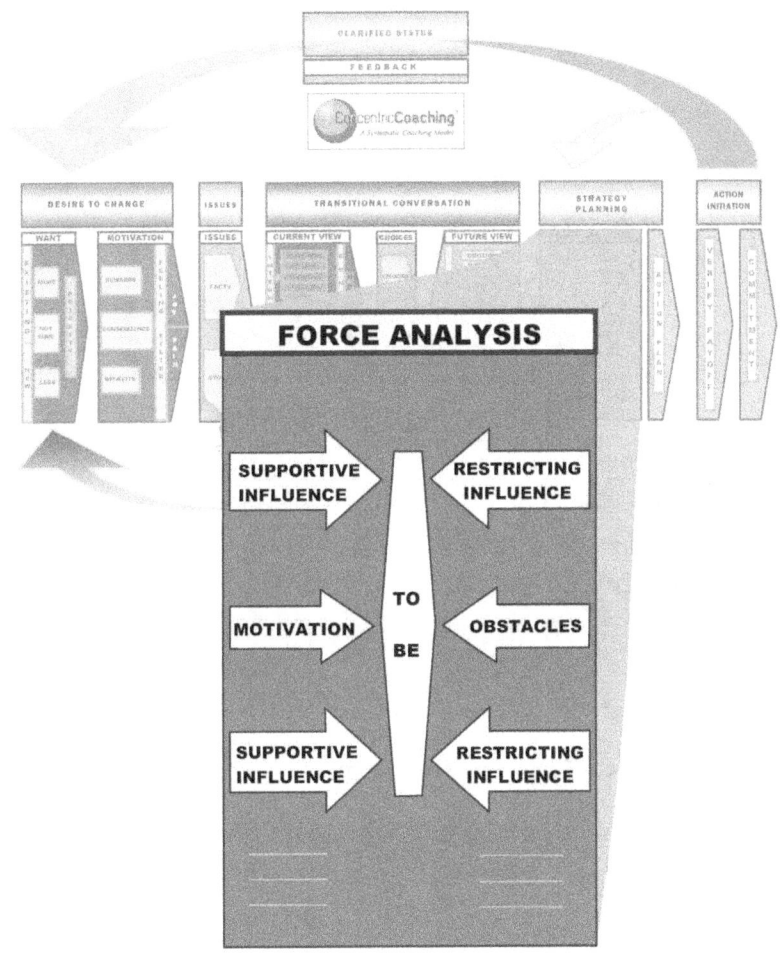

Table of Q-TIP Questions

Support Leading	Support Bridging
1. What about you can support outcome? 2. What external factors support your outcome? 3. Who else would benefit from getting what you want?	7. Statement moves you toward want? 8. What are other supportive influences? 9. What did you learn from that?
Input *Potential action statement* ⇨	**Output** *List of action influences for the selected action statement* ⇨
4. Where might you get in your own way? 5. What external environments hinder outcome? 6. Who or what could be threatened by your success?	10. What are other restricting influences? 11. Any others who might disapprove? 12. Any reason not to move forward?
Obstacle Leading	**Obstacle Bridging**

Intention of the Q-TIPs for this segment:

This segment is all about competing forces; restraining and supportive influences.

The **Input** is the potential action statement; this action statement is the springboard for the consideration of the examination of competing forces.

The **Output** of this segment is a list of action influences for the selected action statement; this is the setup for the development of the action plan in the next segment.

SEGMENT 7: FORCE ANALYSIS
Training & Discussion

1. **Purpose of the Segment**

   a. The purpose of this segment, *FORCE ANALYSIS*, is to identify the selected action statement and those influences, both supportive and restrictive, which affect that action statement.

   b. The contribution of this segment is to get beyond the obvious action or solutions that occur to most clients and to look deeper into the balance of forces which support or obstruct behavior change.

2. **Input**

   a. The input is a potential action statement. This statement contains a brainstormed list of potential actions that might be taken in order to affect the change that supports the identified want.

   b. It is important to carefully consider both internal and external environments in the development of a potential action plan. Without both considerations, it is unlikely that a client will have a clear picture of the forces pushing them forward and pulling them back.

3. **Output**

   a. The output of the *FORCE ANALYSIS* is a list of action influences for the selected action statement.

   b. During the *FORCE ANALYSIS* the coach helps the client explore supportive and restricting influences to the potential action statements. These influences are often numerous and unnoticed by the client. They can include any environment but often fall in the realm of external environments.

4. Guides

a. Supportive Influence: Supportive influences are all of those environments, people...anything which would support the achievement of the want. Supportive influences include the positive aspects of motivation.

b. Restrictive Influence: Restrictive influences are all of those environments, people...anything which would inhibit the achievement of the want. Restrictive influences include the inhibiting aspects of motivation and other obstacles.

c. TO BE: The state of to-be is the summary statement of those influences affecting the selected action statement.

5. Definitions

a. FORCE ANALYSIS: is a brainstorming activity identifying supportive and restricting influences and the selected action statement.

b. Supportive influences: The supportive influences are internal/external environments; to include, values, beliefs and attitudes. These environments are real or perceived, which positively affect the client's perspective toward the selection of a particular action statement.

c. Restricting influences: The restricting influences are internal/external environments; to include, values, beliefs and attitudes. These environments are real or perceived, that push back against (negatively influence) the client's perspective toward the selection of a particular action.

d. TO BE: TO-BE is the ultimate balance of beliefs and environments that would allow for wants to naturally exist.

6. Questions

SUPPORT LEADING

Q-tip #1:   What about you can support outcome?

Expanded question #1: What is it about you that would positively influence or support the actions or results you are considering? What about you would contribute to moving the action statement forward? (This is the internal environment view)

Discussion #1: This question is especially useful with new clients who are unfamiliar with force analysis or where their want is complex and has many potential actions. The new client is often unaware of their own nature or their internal environments. How might their own capabilities provide more support than originally thought?

Q-tip #2:   What external factors support your outcome?

Expanded question #2: Are there any external opportunities or resources which would support your success?

Discussion #2: This question is especially useful with new clients who are unfamiliar with force analysis or where the want is complex and has many potential actions. The opportunities, resources or forms of support are often unexplored or overlooked by clients. There may be people who if asked would be happy to support you.

Q-tip #3:   Who else would benefit from getting what you want?

Expanded question #3: Is there anyone who could benefit from your success? Could they be convinced to help you?

Discussion #3: This is a useful question where client confidence is an issue or where outside support may be valuable. Example: your boss is always frustrated by the head mechanic. He is often late for work and demonstrates a bad attitude to other employees. Unfortunately the boss is reluctant to fire the head mechanic because he is the only person qualified to repair a key piece of equipment. If your client was willing to get trained on the key piece of equipment it would benefit the boss by freeing him from being dependent on the head mechanic with the bad attitude.

OBSTACLE LEADING

Q-tip #4:   Where might you get in your own way?

Expanded question #4: What is it about you that would negatively influence or hinder the actions or results you are considering? Do you have any self-destructive habits which might inhibit your success? Have you ever experienced getting in your own way? What beliefs, attitudes or behaviors contributed to your lack of success?

Discussion #4: This question is useful where the client lacks confidence or lacks a track record of success. This is a good a place for the client to explore oneself and to look for places where they might get in their own way. For example, the client is intimidated by authority figures and may have trouble communicating upward.

Q-tip #5:   What external environments hinder outcome?

Expanded question #5: Are there characteristics of any external environments that might negatively influence or hinder your success? Have you burned any bridges behind you? Are there any people who would not be troubled with your experiencing a failure?

Discussion #5: This question is good for situations with complex external environments involved. This question is used to focus the client on anyone that might influence the outcome of your results. For example, a peer might be jealous of a client's opportunity for promotion, wishing it for themselves.

Q-tip #6:   Who or what could be threatened by your success?

Expanded question #6: Who or what would be indirectly hurt or threatened by you success? How might they be hurt?

Discussion #6: Change, either real or perceived, often threatens people. This is a good general question used to help the client explore threats. For example, peers might be concerned that they will have to pick up some of the clients workload while he is in training for a promotion. Exploring this question with the client can help the client develop a considerate and sensitive strategy for eliminating the perceived fear experienced by peers.

SUPPORT BRIDGING

Q-tip #7: **Statement move you toward want?**

Expanded question #7: Which action statement will move you most effectively toward your want?

Discussion #7: This question is all about priorities and decision making. It's time for the client to start selecting their highest priority action statement. The client is moving from <u>potential</u> action statements…to the <u>selected</u> action statement.

Q-tip #8: **What are other supportive influences?**

Expanded question #8: Can you think of any other supportive influences which might affect your <u>selected</u> action statement?

Discussion #8: This question is designed to identify any remaining supportive influences which might affect the selected action statement. At this point, the client should be able to list <u>all</u> supportive influences.

(Coach's Note This is a summary question, there may not be any new information presented. However, the point is that the client should be able to literally list all relevant and significant supportive influences, for use in the next segment, ACTION PLAN.)

Q-tip #9:   What did you learn from that?

Expanded question #9: Now that you have identified the desired output, what did you learn from that…about yourself, your capabilities? How can you use this new information in the future?

Discussion #9: It is important to the client to acknowledge any moment of awareness or achievement…and why that awareness/achievement is important. This will permit the client to transport this new skill of realization to other opportunities throughout the process. The real question is….what did the client learn that is unique to this segment?

OBSTACLE BRIDGING

Question #10:   What are other restricting influences?

Expanded question #10: Can you think of any other restricting influences which might affect your <u>selected</u> action statement?

Discussion #10: This question is designed to identify any remaining restricting influences which might affect the selected action statement. At this point, the client should be able to list <u>all</u> restricting influences.

(Coach's Note: This is a summary question, there may not be any new information presented. However, the point is that the client should be able to literally list all relevant and significant restricting influences, for use in the next segment, ACTION PLAN.)

Q-tip #11:   Any others who might disapprove?

Expanded question #11: Conduct an enviro-scan; is there any one else who might not approve of your selected action statement?

Discussion #11: The client is continuously challenged to determine if there is anyone or anything which might inhibit the achievement of the desired want. Asking a question like this often stimulates an additional consideration or thought. You don't want to go into overkill; sometimes this question might be asked quickly, perhaps even casually. It's just providing an opportunity for the client to get all restrictions on the table.

Q-tip #12: Any reason not to move forward?

Expanded question #12: Can you think of any reason not to move forward?

Discussion #12: Similar to the above question, this question provides the client with an opportunity to stop the process, reconsider their want, or make the firm decision to continue forward. Similar again to the previous question, do not make a huge deal out of this question and use it judiciously. Ask the question, get the response, and move on.

SEGMENT 8: ACTION PLAN

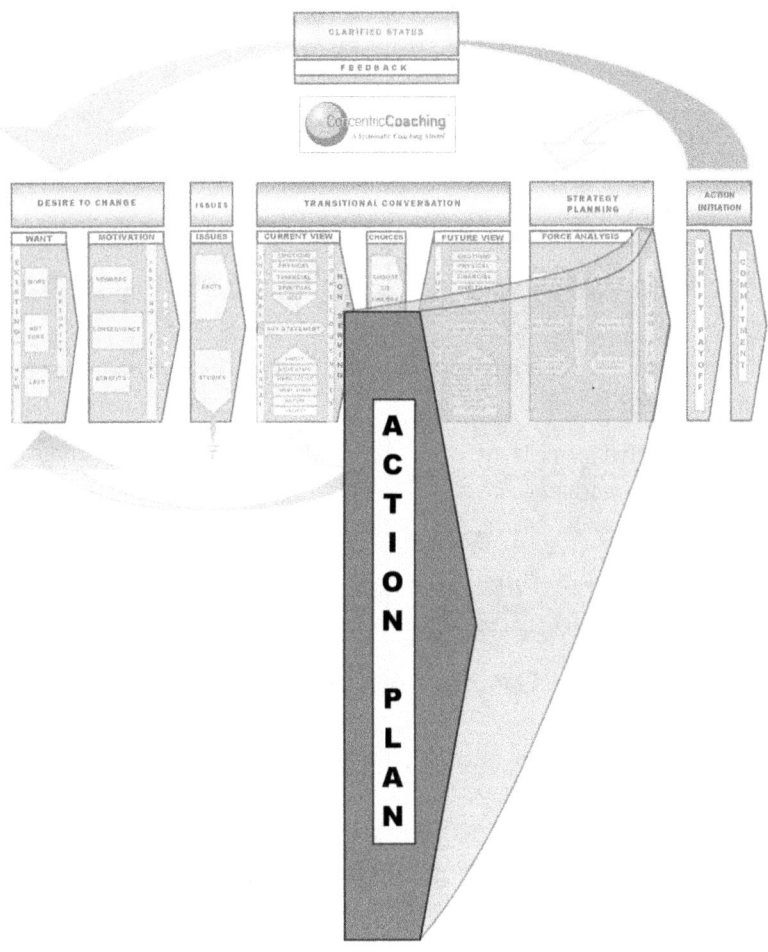

Table of Q-TIP Questions

Support Leading	Support Bridging
1. How utilize supportive influences? 2. What are the action steps? 3. How prioritize the action steps?	7. What is the time line? 8. Ready to write the action plan? 9. What did you learn from that?
Input *List of action influences for the selected action* ⇨	**Output** Action Plan ⇨
4. What influence might stop you? 5. How manage restricting influences? 6. Anyone else's priority precludes yours?	10. Any problems with an action plan? 11. Still on board with action plan? 12. Anything else?
Obstacle Leading	**Obstacle Bridging**

Intention of the Q-TIPs for this segment:

This segment is all about action…deciding to do something on purpose…and getting to it.

The **Input** is a list of action influences for the selected action statement; this information sets the stage for the construction of the plan.

The **Output** of this segment is the action plan; the action plan is the true beginning of actually accomplishing the want.

SEGMENT 8: ACTION PLAN
Training & Discussion

1. **Purpose of the segment**

   a. The purpose of the *ACTION PLAN* is to produce a workable plan of action or actions.

   b. It is at this point that the environments have been considered, the force analysis has been evaluated, and it's time to put together a comprehensive (relevant to the desired want) action plan.

   c. It is important to keep the depth and complexity of the action plan consistent with the desired want. For example, you don't need a 20-page action plan to decide to talk with you boss about a raise.

2. **Input**

   a. The input to the *ACTION PLAN* segment is a list of action influences for the selected action statement

3. **Output**

   a. The output from the *ACTION PLAN* segment is the action plan.

4. **Guides**

   a. There are no guides in this segment

5. **Definitions**

   a. Action: An action is not just a philosophical position, it's not even an action plan. An action is implementing or executing a decision. Typically, action requires the client to conduct an observable (and accountable) behavior.

b. Action plan: An action plan is the appropriately detailed list of actions, sub-actions, milestones, outcomes and scheduling for a series of sequenced actions. Completing an action plan presumes achievement of the desired goal.

6. Questions

SUPPORT LEADING

Q-tip #1: How utilize supportive influences?

Expanded question #1: In what way do you envision utilizing the supportive influences to accomplish your action statement?

Discussion #1: This is the first step in the development of the action plan. The client needs to figure out what to do with the supportive influences. Specifically, the client needs to accommodate the supportive influences in the development of the action steps.

Q-tip #2: What are the action steps?

Expanded question #2: What are the action steps necessary to accomplish the selected action statement?

Discussion #2: This can be a brainstorming exercise. The point of the question is to cause the client to consider all of the steps necessary to achieve the action statement.
It's important that the client realize (same with the coach) that not all action statements require a 10-page document to describe. Frequently, the desired action requires one step...with a simple time line.

(Coach's Note: You need to consider to restricting influences prior to performing this step).

Q-tip #3:   How prioritize the action steps?

Expanded question #3: How would you prioritize the action steps?

Discussion #3: Once the action steps have been developed, the steps need to be prioritized and sequenced by the <u>client</u>.

OBSTACLE LEADING

Q-tip #4:   What influence might stop you?

Expanded question #4: Do you perceive of any restricting influences which would <u>stop</u> the achievement of your want? Which actions will you struggle with or resist.

Discussion #4: This question is designed to be provocative and abrupt. At the same time, it is designed to cause the client to quickly review all of the influences and make a judgment about their ability to continue toward the achievement of their want. There are two paths: (1) there is an obstacle which can't be overcome or (2) the client becomes overwhelmed and just can't move forward.

Q-tip #5:   How manage restricting influences?

Expanded question #5: In what way do you envision managing the restricting influences in the accomplishment your action statement? How will you make these actions easier?

Discussion #5: This step is necessary to be performed prior to the development of the action steps. This is another brainstorming activity. It's important for the client to realize that influences typically can't be eliminated as much as managed. This step in the process is designed to allow the client to confidently accommodate those influences which are not within their control.

Q-tip #6:   Anyone else's priority preclude yours?

Expanded question #6: Would anyone else's priorities preclude your reaching your want?

Discussion #6: This question is all about people. Are there any people significant to you who have a priority that you need to accommodate? It's not that your needs aren't important as much as the other person need to take a higher position in your life.
(Coach's Note: Challenge if this is a real higher priority or if this is a default position by the client of putting others first...automatically.)

SUPPORT BRIDGING

Q-tip #7: What is the time line?

Expanded question #7: What do you envision the time line to be for the performance and completion of the action steps?

Discussion #7: Once the action steps have been developed, the steps need to be prioritized, sequenced, and then a schedule needs to be applied. Ensure that the time line accommodates the reality of work, home and other environments. Additionally, make sure the time line isn't so aggressive that the slightest bump in the system causes it to crash.

(Coach's Note: Make sure the client is clear as to the difference between important and urgent.)

Q-tip #8: Ready to write the action plan?

Expanded question #8: Are your ready to write the action plan?

Discussion #8: This is a call to action. It's time to actually write the action plan. Remember that not all action statements require a large and complex plan. Sometimes it's just a matter of doing it without the drama. A good habit for simple actions might be to just list the action steps in your day planner or calendar. Keep the actions in perspective.

Q-tip #9:   What did you learn from that?

Expanded question #9: Now that you have identified the desired output, what did you learn from that...about yourself, your capabilities? How can you use this new information in the future?

Discussion #9: This is a question which can be asked at the end of each segment. It is important to the client to acknowledge any moment of awareness or achievement...and why that awareness/achievement is important. This will permit the client to transport this new skill of realization to other opportunities throughout the process. The real question is....what did the client learn that is unique to this segment?

OBSTACLE BRIDGING

Q-tip #10:   Any problems with an action plan?

Expanded question #10: Do you have any problems with developing and living with an action plan?

Discussion #10: This question has two aspects: (1) developing an action plan and (2) living with an action plan. Some people have a problem with the regimentation of a written action plan. Again, not all action plans require a detailed and complex action plan. Sometimes it's a simple set of action steps. At the same time, other clients may have a problem with working the plan. They can make all the lists and write the plan, but then have a problem with failure to complete a plan. At the same time, they may have a problem with success. This is an opportunity to address either side of this issue.

Q-tip #11:   Still on board with action plan?

Expanded question #11: Are you still on board with developing and actually doing an action plan?

Discussion #11: This question is all about confidence and intention. It is a question the coach might ask the client just before actually writing the formal action plan. This implies the intent of both developing and implementing the plan.

Q-tip #12:   Anything else?
Expanded question #12: Last chance, is there anything else that you need to include in the action plan?

Discussion #12: Ok, the client has examined all influences, the steps have been developed, the steps were prioritized and sequenced, the time schedule was completed and the plan was written...is there anything else that the coach or the client can think of that needs to be included?

A lot of work went into the development of this action plan....take some time to celebrate with the client. Not cheerlead, but genuinely applaud the client.

SEGMENT 9: VERIFY PAYOFF

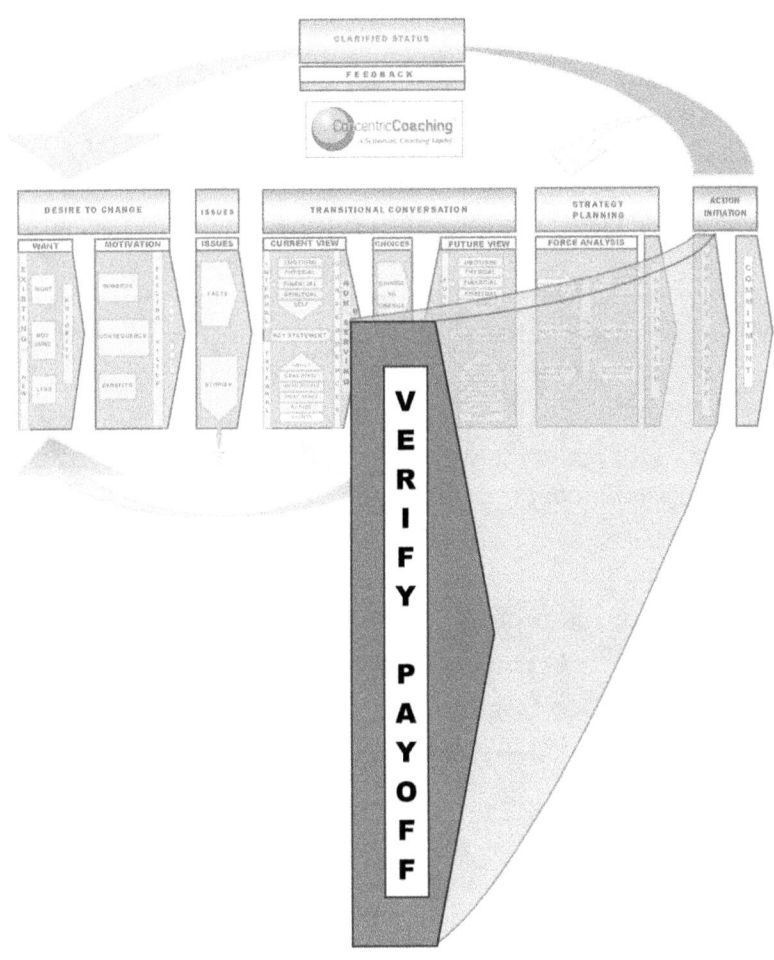

Table of Q-TIP Questions

Support Leading	Support Bridging
1. What would excite you about doing this action? 2. Will you be at peace with the endpoint? 3. How do you feel about your chances of winning this?	7. Will this win benefit anyone else? 8. How much bigger is the payoff than the cost to change? 9. What did you learn from that?
Input Action Plan ⇨	**Output** Reinforced payoff(s) for the action plan ⇨
4. What would get in the way of your excitement (externally)? 5. What would get in the way of your excitement (internally)? 6. What about this action would make you proud?	10. Is this a short term/long term win? 11. How will you sustain this win? 12. Would you regret this action if you didn't "win" the payoff?
Obstacle Leading	**Obstacle Bridging**

Intention of the Q-TIPs for this segment:

This segment is all about the payoff...identifying how you would win by completing the action plan.

The **Input** is an action plan; this information sets the stage for the construction of the plan.

The **Output** of this segment is the reinforced payoff(s) for the action plan; this is the list of reasons for actually completing the action plan.

SEGMENT 9: VERIFY PAYOFF
Training & Discussion

1. **Purpose of the Segment**

   a. The purpose of the *VERIFY PAYOFF* segment is to ensure that the client fully understands the payoff for achieving the action plan.

   b. The payoff, in particular, needs to be clearly specified in that the payoff is really the motivation behind making the change. Frankly, if there is no clear reason for making the change…if there is no win…why should the behavior be changed?

   c. It is important for the coach to hear the client say why they want to accomplish this change and what the client will get out of making the effort. Do not let the client gloss over this particular step.

2. **Input**

   a. The input to this segment is the action plan.

   b. As with many of the other segments, it is important that the action plan be clearly specified in order to define motivation and payoff.

3. **Output**

   a. The output to this segment is the reinforced payoff(s) for the action plan.

   b. Again, the assumption is that, with the payoff or motivation properly identified, the action plan <u>will</u> be implemented.

4. Guides

a. There are no guides within this segment.

5. Definitions

a. Payoff: The payoff is the increase in positive feedback or decrease in negative feedback in some manner.

b. Motivation: Motivation is simply the call to action, something that will cause the client to move forward. Hopefully, with careful management by the coach, the client will have in place environments which will sustain and maintain the momentum of the client.

Regarding the questions to follow:

(Coach's Note: Many of these questions might seem like commitment questions. In truth, what the coach needs to do is keep the conversation fairly light around what seems to be commitment and guide the conversation toward the benefit and payoff of the action. Different than commitment, part of the payoff is emotional, such as how I feel about taking the desired action, as well as the obvious outcome.)

6. Questions

SUPPORT LEADING

Q-tip #1:   What would excite you about doing this action?

Expanded question #1: Why are you taking this action? Does it make you happy? What would excite you about doing this?

Discussion #1: This question is all about internal motivation. It's about the payoff....the reward for doing what the client wants to do anyway...but could use some acknowledgement of what will be the outcome of the effort.

Q-tip #2:   Will you be at peace with the endpoint?

Expanded question #2: If you get what you want, if you achieve the win that you desire....will you be at peace with the endpoint? Does the statement of the action plan provide a sense of relief or is it a new source of tension?

Discussion #2: This is a consequence question. This question helps determine the boundary of the prospective action. This question is also about calmness and joy. Does the client even know what it means to be at peace with a decision or action? (**Coach's Note: Lots of room for inner discovery with this question.**)

Q-tip #3:   How do you feel about your chances of winning this?

Expanded question #3: What about your action plan would make you feel like this is a winning strategy? Do you feel like success is likely?

Discussion #3: The question goes to the heart of the client; do they think that what they carefully plan is likely to succeed? This entire conversation is designed to be supportive, not challenging or based in obstacle.

OBSTACLE LEADING

Q-tip #4:   What would get in the way of your excitement (externally)?

Expanded question #4: You seem to be having a tough time visualizing the happy part of the completion of this effort; is there anything or anyone around you who you believe would get in the way of your excitement?

Discussion #4: This question is designed to bring the client into their head.... thinking about fully experiencing the emotions associated with completing their effort. The primary focus in this question is the external component. This might be a good time for another external environments scan.

Q-tip #5:   What would get in the way of your excitement (internally)?

Expanded question #5: You seem to be having a tough time visualizing the happy part of the completion of this effort; what is stopping you from experiencing that excitement? Have you had a happy ending to an effort before? How did you show that happiness? How would it <u>feel</u> to feel happy...even if it's just to yourself?

Discussion #5: This question is designed to bring the client into their head.... thinking about experiencing the joy of that completion. The primary focus in this question is the internal component. This might be a good time for another internal environments scan.

Q-tip #6:   What about this action would make you proud?

Expanded question #6: Would you be proud if: you did exactly as you planned...if everything turned out perfectly...if everyone that <u>could</u> benefit from your efforts got what you planned? Who else would be proud of your efforts?

Discussion #6: This question is designed to be extremely emotional. This question is not supposed to elicit a clinical list of proud people. It's more about the internal pride that comes from doing something well. More importantly, it's about taking that critical moment to fully internalize what it means to do a good thing...and acknowledge having done that good thing.

SUPPORT BRIDGING

Q-tip #7:   Will this win benefit anyone else?

Expanded question #7: Review your environments; if you win, who else or what will also win? Are you excited that someone else might win as well? In what way could you make it an even bigger win for them?

Discussion #7: This question is the flip side of who loses if the client wins. The question is….if the client wins…who else wins? One payoff for the client is if someone else wins; the question is…how can the client maximize that win for the other person…ultimately benefiting themselves.

Q-tip #8:   How much bigger is the payoff than the cost to change?

Expanded question #8: Is there any way to make the payoff even bigger than you had originally thought? Your wildest dreams!! How big is this for you?

Discussion #8: This question is all about expanding what the client thinks about what may be. It's not about cheerleading; it's about serious (maybe fun) expansion of the client through their own glass ceiling.

This should be a launching question; the question that is asked of the client just before commitment.

Q-tip #9:   What did you learn from that?

Expanded question #9: Now that you have identified the desired output, what did you learn from that…about yourself, your capabilities? How can you use this new information in the future?

Discussion #9: This is a question which can be asked at the end of each segment. It is important to the client to acknowledge any moment of awareness or achievement…and why that awareness/achievement is important. This will permit the client to transport this new skill of realization to other opportunities throughout the process. The real question is….what did the client learn that is unique to this segment?

OBSTACLE BRIDGING

Q-tip #10:   Is this a short term/long term win?

Expanded question #10: Is this a short term win or are you taking the longer view? How does this perception impact the enduring performance?

(Coach's Note: Don't forget, sometimes a short term solution is precisely what is needed!! Don't confuse a short term strategic decision with an instant gratification situation.)

Discussion #10: This question is all about the emotions connected with taking the long or short term view. Additionally, the conversation might address the perceived benefits of both views.

Q-tip #11: How will you sustain this win?

Expanded question #11: Is the path too long for a win? Where will the energy come from to achieve the win? Is the win crashing over the finish line or is the win sustainable? And how will all of this make you feel?

Discussion #11: This is a harder question than a coach might think. This question is all about the emotions of the longer view. It's easy for a client to talk about how they might feel about a short term effort; however, it's much more difficult to find that place which describes how the client might feel over the long haul.

Q-tip #12: Would you regret this action if you didn't win the payoff?

Expanded question #12: What if there was only a small chance of a positive payoff? Is the payoff valuable for you? Is this one of those situations where just knowing you're doing something feels good?

Discussion #12: This question is all about the ability of the client to acknowledge the emotions associated with failure or a diminished win. Additionally, watch out for a negative (vs. joyous) perspective that the client may bring to this conversation. It could be an indication of a resistance to the change, a fear, or a lack of confidence in the strategy or their ability.

SEGMENT 10: COMMITMENT

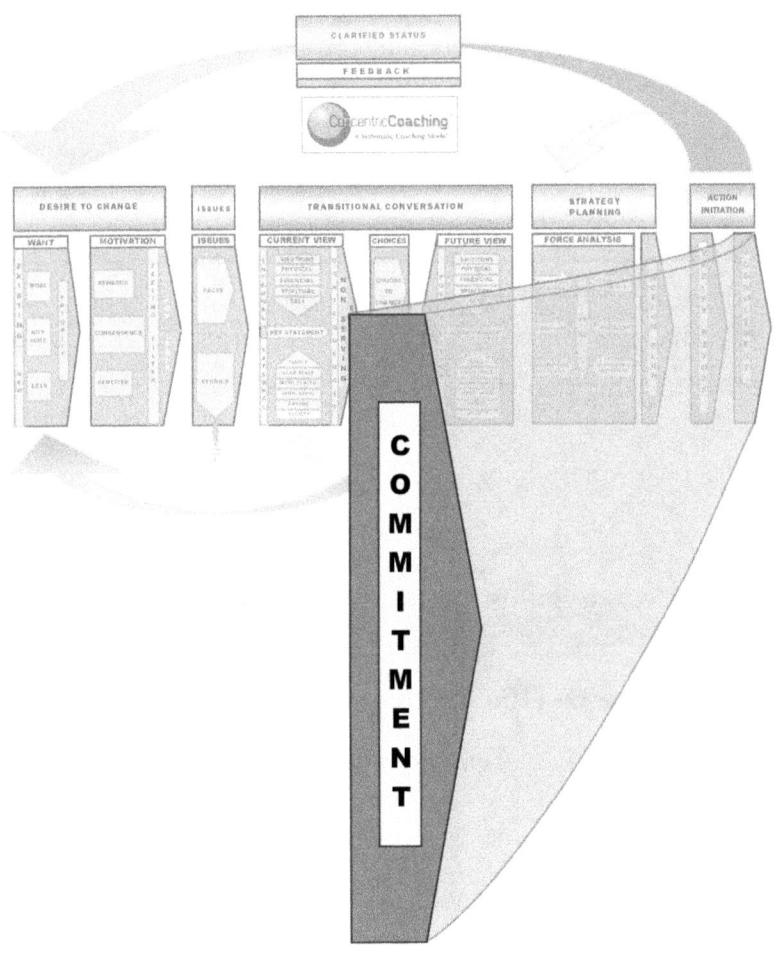

Table of Q-TIP Questions

Support Leading	Support Bridging
1. Are you clear what the action plan is? 2. Do you trust the action plan strategy? 3. Are the payoffs clear?	7. Anything left to talk about? 8. Have you decided to work the plan? 9. What did you learn from that?
Input *Reinforced payoff(s) for the action plan* ⇨	**Output** *Commitment to implementing the action plan* ⇨
4. Is there anything to stop you (externally)? 5. Is there anything to stop you (internally)? 6. Is this plan worth doing?	10. Commitment been a problem in past? 11. How would you FEEL if the action failed? 12. How feel about failure in the past?
Obstacle Leading	**Obstacle Bridging**

Intention of the Q-TIPs for this segment:

This segment is all about commitment…is it time for you to do your action plan?

The **Input** is a reinforced payoff(s) for the action plan; you know what to do, how you will benefit…now it's time to get ready to commit.

The **Output** of this segment is the commitment to implementing the action plan; it's time to go.

SEGMENT 10: COMMITMENT
Training & Discussion

1. **Purpose of the Segment**

   a. The purpose of the segment, *COMMITMENT*, is all about good strategies, belief in the strategy, and that the reward is greater than the cost...and finally, committing to actually implementing the action plan.

   b. The trick to making a commitment is to have the discipline to finish what you set out to accomplish. By discipline, what is meant is not beating yourself with a whip... it is more about asking yourself, "If I have the skill and I really want to do this thing....can I"? If the answer is yes....and you apply yourself appropriately...then you have the discipline to do the task.

   c. Lastly, the client's belief and management of failure may be examined, as necessary. It's important to identify and work with the client to manage any resistance to moving forward.

2. **Input**

   a. The input to this segment is the specified payoff for the action plan.

   b. This means that the client has selected an action plan, has identified those environments which will hinder or support the performance, has measured the payoff for the performance and is ready to make the commitment to actually accomplishing the plan.

3. **Output**

   a. The output from this segment, the commitment to an action plan, is more than just a mental decision. It is the preparation necessary to actually pursuing the plan. The plan now has a focus....and the accomplishment of it is at hand.

b. It should be noted that this segment does not mean to imply that every goal has to be a production. Not everything requires a military level plan. However, it has been observed that NOT having a plan...even the most simplistic of plans....is a clear indicator of the lower likelihood of meeting your desired outcome.

4. Guides

a. There are no guides within this segment.

5. Definitions

a. Commitment: Commitment is the decision to act and <u>complete</u> an action.

b. Trust: Trust is a measure of predictability.

6. Questions

SUPPORT LEADING

Q-tip #1:   Are you clear what the action plan is?

Expanded question #1: You've decided what to change, you've run the goal through your environments and through the strategy planning process...are you clear about all of the steps and measures of your action plan?

Discussion #1: These questions are the concluding questions used to examine the last steps before committing to a course of action. In this case, it's important for the coach to ensure that the client has a clear idea of what they want to do...in clear, definable, achievable terms.

Q-tip #2:   Do you trust the action plan strategy?

Expanded question #2: You know <u>what</u> you want...now, do you know exactly <u>how</u> you're going to accomplish your goal? And, more importantly, do you trust your own strategy?

Discussion #2: The next step in the process: the client knows the goal...now, how about the steps to get there...the schedule....the strategy. Again, in clear, achievable steps.

(Coach's Note: This is supposed to be a supportive series of question...not trying to decrease the client's self confidence. Try to keep the conversation upbeat, encouraging, and ultimately, positive.)

Q-tip #3:   Are the payoffs clear?

Expanded question #3: Do you know what the benefits of accomplishing your goal are? Can you say what the payoffs are? Are the payoffs clear?

Discussion #3: This is a summarizing question; not an initial examination of payoffs. The client knows what to do....and how to do it....now, the question for the coach/client is...are the payoffs clear and sufficient. Is it clear to the client why the goal is to be reached?

OBSTACLE LEADING

Q-tip #4:   Is there anything to stop you (externally)?

Expanded question #4: Can you think of anything which might impede or stop you from accomplishing your action plan? Is it worth running quickly over the environments to double check? Who can provide emotional support to help you with your task during the performance of this plan? If you take all of the action plan steps, can you envision any way that your strategy will fail?

Discussion #4: The steps and payoff are clear...now, are there any external resisting influences...any external environments which are not considered which might hinder the client from achieving the goal.

Q-tip #5:   Is there anything to stop you (internally)?

Expanded question #5: As a final check, are you ready to continue? Is there any internal reason why you shouldn't move forward?

Discussion #5: This question is about the client internally. Is the client mentally, physically, emotionally, spiritually, ready to take the next step?

Q-tip #6:   Is this plan worth doing?

Expanded question #6: As a final check, is this plan worth doing?

Discussion #6: From the obstacle quadrant, are there any reasons why the client shouldn't implement the action plan....does the action plan help the client more toward their want?

SUPPORT BRIDGING

Q-tip #7:   Is there anything left to talk about?

Expanded question #7: You've stated that the action plan strategy is good, the plan is doable, and the reward are sufficient to make the action worthwhile. (With no judgment at all) is there anything that we need to talk about before you begin the action plan?

Discussion #7: This question is just a reality check and is the final question before (hopefully) the client says with all joy and enthusiasm....yes, let's do it!!

Q-tip #8:   Have you decided to work the plan?

Expanded question #8: Have you decided to work the plan?

Discussion #8: There are only two answers to this question: Yes or other. If it's a weak yes or other, it's the same as a no. Obviously, if it's not yes, there is an opportunity to explore the client's ability to commit.

Q-tip #9:   What did you learn from that?

Expanded question #9: Now that you have identified the desired output, what did you learn from that....about yourself, your capabilities? How can you use this new information in the future?

Discussion #9: This is a question which can be asked at the end of each segment. It is important to the client to acknowledge any moment of awareness or achievement...and why that awareness/achievement is important. This will permit the client to transport this new skill of realization to other opportunities throughout the process. The real question is....what did the client learn that is unique to this segment?

OBSTACLE BRIDGING

Question #10: Commitment been a problem in the past?

Expanded question #10: Have you ever had a problem with commitment before? When? Why? What happened? What was the consequence of that missed commitment?

Discussion #10: This question is designed to address commitment problems with the client. It is meant to be a constructive question, rather than confrontational. In some cases, the client doesn't even consciously acknowledge a problem with commitment...however, they just never seem to get going.

Q-tip #11:   How would you FEEL if the action failed?

Expanded question #11: What would you do if you tried your hardest...and the effort just failed?

Discussion #11: This question might never be asked or might be asked in the event of hesitancy or overconfidence. If you do decide to explore this emotion, be careful that the client doesn't collapse into this feeling. Make sure that the session ends on a more positive note...don't let the client dwell on this aspect of the action plan. Continue the process through the failure....how the client felt...How that learning will apply to the current situation...and how what was learned will minimize the impact on this new action plan. End on a position of greater expectation and enthusiasm.

Q-tip #12:   How feel about failure in the past?

Expanded question #12: How have you typically responded when failing in the past?

Discussion #12: The types of answers expected here are primarily behavioral. How did I act, feel, respond when experiencing a failure? Can the client even say the word? Does the client begin story telling? Does the client react even to the anticipation of failure? This might be the place to help the client insert additional support.

Be careful to not move into therapy at this point.!! Keep the client facing forward. We're not looking for root cause with coaching; coaching is about the forward view. "I understand where you are coming from...now, how can you use that information to move toward your want?"

SEGMENT 11: FEEDBACK

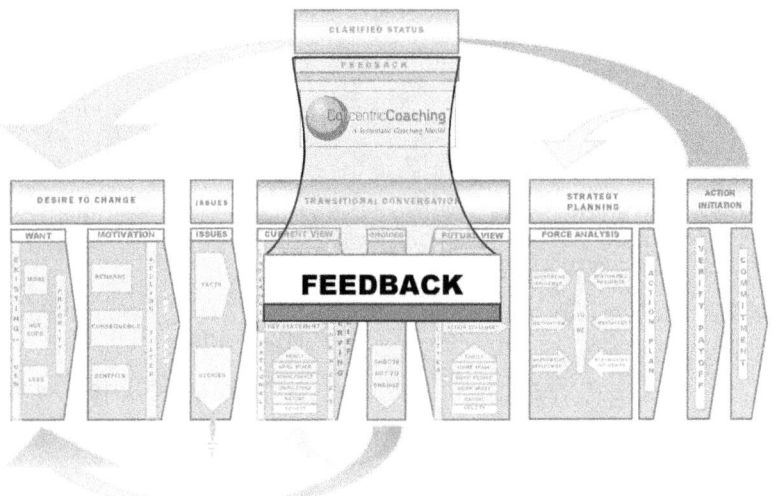

Table of Q-TIP Questions

Support Leading		Support Bridging	
1. How did you do? 2. What worked for you? 3. What succeeded wildly?		7. What do you want to do next? 8. How does it feel to win? 9. What did you learn from that?	
Input *Commitment to implementing the action plan*	⇨	**Output** *Desired change*	⇨
4. What didn't get done? 5. What didn't work? 6. What can you learn from a failure?		10. Is it time to rethink your plan? 11. Could your wants have changed? 12. Is it time for a new want?	
Obstacle Leading		Obstacle Bridging	

Intention of the Q-TIPs for this segment:

This segment is all about …well, doing your action plan. How is it going?

The **Input** is a commitment to implementing the action plan; you've committed, you've worked on it…now it's time to see how you did.

The **Output** of this segment is the desired change; so….how DID it go?

SEGMENT 11: FEEDBACK
Training & Discussion

1. Purpose of the Segment

a. The purpose of the *FEEDBACK* segment is to continue the coaching and behavior change process within the concentric methodology.

b. Once an action plan has been determined, the payoff has been determined and, most importantly, the commitment to make the change has been made....it is time to trust and verify.

c. Trust and verify means that the outcome of the commitment is presumed to take place, but there still needs to be checks and balances to ensure that the behavior change truly takes place.

d. Therefore, there are four alternative paths that a client may follow: (a) the action plan is completed and the client may select a new want or end the coaching, (b) the action plan is in progress and the client will continue working on the current plan, (c) the action plan is not meeting the client's wants and the client revises the plan, or (d) the client has a new higher priority and postpones the feedback conversation in order to work on the new want.

e. Revising the action plan is probably the most frequent change that a client will make to an action plan. Be careful of the paralysis of analysis!! Hold the client (appropriately) accountable for making a plan and sticking to it. However, this is not to say that a plan shouldn't be changed...just that it should be changed for a good reason.

f. Accounting for an incremental change in behavior is actually the big win. Long lasting behavior change comes from incremental change...so, reporting and accounting for progress toward a goal is to be celebrated. This is the time for applauding the client....and make sure the client fully embraces the achievement as well. Similarly, accounting for a lack of performance should be assessed and dealt with as well. Is the client moving toward the goal? Monitoring their own behaviors and environments? Following the plan? Does the plan need to be modified...if so, how?

g. Finally, the plan has been constructed....followed....and it's time for a new want. Don't forget to celebrate the conclusion of one phase of life before leaping headlong into the next step....make sure that both you AND the client appreciate the work that went into that change....and celebrate it!!

2. Input

a. The input to the *FEEDBACK* segment is a commitment to implementing the action plan.

b. This means that the client has constructed an action plan, has verified the payoff, and most importantly, has committed to the pursuit of that action plan.

3. Output

a. The output from the *FEEDBACK* segment is the pursuit of the desired change. To arrive at the desired change, the client and the coach need to explore the results of the implemented action plan.

b. This exploration will lead to the achievement of one of the four paths described in the purpose section; completing the concentric nature of this coaching conversation.

4. Guides

a. There are no guides in this segment.

5. Definitions

a. Revise: Revising a plan is different from being afraid of a particular action. Revise means to modify or change. Change shouldn't be the last resort of the client. It should be a progressive step...not a defensive maneuver.

b. "DO": As in "How did you do?" is a question based on action, not intent. It's important to focus your intentions and clearly define what you want to do...even intend to do. However, at this stage, it's even more important to DO rather than merely intend. At this point, the question is really....of what you said you were going to DO....how did you DO?

6. Questions

SUPPORT LEADING

Q-tip #1: How did you do?

Expanded question #1: You've worked on your plan for a while now; so, is your plan working for you? How did you actually do?

Discussion #1: In this case, the action plan has been developed and the client is committed to the action. The coach needs to hold the client accountable for their action plan (after asking permission during the previous session). The questions are designed to elicit the status of action taken. It's not about defense. It's not about checking up. It's about the objective view of what was done.

Q-tip #2: What worked for you?

Expanded question #2: You have worked on your action plan for a while; how well has it worked for you?

Discussion #2: This question is best used after the action plan has been functioning for a session or two. Typically it's difficult to see the benefits to any plan immediately after starting it. Frequently, the client begins to see the value of the plan after a few sessions.

This question is designed to get the client out of their heads and develop the communications skills necessary to describe, objectively, not just what they did....but what aspect of what they did worked. This information may be used later in the process to describe past successes.

Q-tip #3:   What succeeded wildly?

Expanded question #3: Did anything you accomplished exceed even your expectations? Did anything just seem to go right? Did anything exceed your expectations wildly?

Discussion #3: This question is all about exceeding expectations. Did the client meet their desired action step/plan? Did the client exceed their expectations? Did the client EXCEED their expectations? It's important to look at not only the achievement but the process of achieving.

OBSTACLE LEADING

Q-tip #4:   What didn't get done?

Expanded question #4: So, did you complete what you committed to from the last session? Let's review what was to be accomplished by this session. Let's then talk about what you did to accomplish that action step/goal. Next, let's find out what didn't get done.

Discussion #4: This question is an ongoing question...and it's all about curiosity. It's all about genuine interest in the client. How have they

been doing on THEIR action plan/step? This is not about monitoring their performance...it's about helping them stay accountable...as THEY need it....to their plan.

Q-tip #5:   What didn't work?

Expanded question #5: You've done the work, you've made the changes…you've walked the walk. Is there any part of the plan that didn't work as you had hoped?

Discussion #5: This is a necessary question at the end or during a steady state condition of a behavioral change. It's important that the client take a look back and see what could have been done easier, better, different…. anything that would make the next action statement more likely to work. Inherent in this review is learning; learning what you did right…learning what you did wrong…and learning what to do better the next time.

Q-tip #6:   What can you learn from a failure?

Expanded question #6: You tried and it didn't work…..what can you learn from this failure?

Discussion #6: This question is not said in the sense of the person being a failure…however, EVERYONE fails upon occasion. It is important to have the client truly know that failure is just a step on the way to success. You have to try….fail….LEARN….try… succeed!! The question is….did the client learn? If so….what was learned?

SUPPORT BRIDGING

Q-tip #7:   What do you want to do next?

Expanded question #7: You've succeeded or things didn't work out as expected? What would you like to do now?

Discussion #7: This question is about having the client objectively view their recent actions and deciding what to do next. This is a good time for being supportive…but letting the client think for themselves. It's important to be objective. There is an old management saying: Trust and Verify. Accept what the client says as true…then have the client provide evidence of their success.

Q-tip #8:   How does it feel to win?

Expanded question #8: How does it feel to have won? To have finished an effort or project? How does your body feel <u>right now</u>? How are you celebrating your win? With whom?

Discussion #8: This is a dig deeper question. This is not a flippant question but a question that goes to the heart of the client completing a step or plan. This question is all about the feeling...not just reporting in. It is important as well to not rush through this question....allow time for the question to percolate. Also, listen for how the client acknowledges his/her successes. Are they comfortable with saying out loud what they have done? Do they ignore the need to celebrate...even in the smallest way?

Q-tip #9:   What did you learn from that?

Expanded question #9: Now that you have identified the desired output, what did you learn from that? About yourself, your capabilities? How can you use this new information in the future?

Discussion #9: This is a question which can be asked at the end of each segment. It is important to the client to acknowledge any moment of awareness or achievement...and why that awareness/achievement is important. This will permit the client to transport this new skill of realization to other opportunities throughout the process. The real question is....what did the client learn that is unique to this segment?

OBSTACLE BRIDGING

Q-tip #10:   Is it time to rethink your plan?

Expanded question #10: You've worked on your plan for a while and (with concurrence from the client) you seem to be having trouble moving forward; is this the time to rethink your plan? Is this the right time to be doing this plan? Is it still the right want?

Discussion #10: This set of questions is designed to determine if the client needs to reconstruct their action plan. Discuss redirecting the efforts of the client back to redesigning the want and continuing through the process. As a coach, it is important that you determine the root cause of the difficulty and work it out with the client. Don't let the client evade actually working the plan without a good reason (their reason).

Q-tip #11:   Could your wants have changed?

Expanded question #11: You seem to be having trouble with your action plan, could it be that you want to adjust your wants? Could something in your life have changed? Has what initially excited you about your want/action plan changed? Has the payoff changed? Do you, perhaps, have a more realistic view of what you want to accomplish?

Discussion #11: This question is designed to differentiate between a redesign of the action plan (implying the same want but a different plan) and a changed want (implying a new want, starting from the beginning). Additionally, be careful that you're not letting the client off the hook for not putting in the necessary effort.

Q-tip #12:   Is it time for a new want?

Expanded question #12: You've successfully completed (and celebrated) the completion of your action plan, is it time for a new want?

Discussion #12: This is the best of all situations. The client has learned how to design and carry through on an action plan...and it's time for something new to work on. In this case, the coach returns back to at the *WANT* segment and continues forward...to a new client with a new behavior. Yahoo!!

OBSERVATIONS

This section is all about the observations that have made through the use of the CCS™ system over the last few years.

Segment 1
I have observed that:

... when a proposed want is explored a different want frequently results.

...most clients want a thing (pay increase of 10%)...rather than an exploration of themselves (how I feel about money).

Segment 2
I have observed that:

...people seem to want to minimize pain....rather than the preferred increase in joy.

... people get excited (motivated) when they have a clear goal (want) in mind.

Segment 3
I have observed that:

... people get lost in their stories and get stuck where they are using the story as a shield or a sword.

...facts are harder to list than are stories. They've lived with stories so long...stories are more fun to tell than to list the true facts.

Segment 4
I have observed that:

... that people tend to focus more on the external issues (environments) because it's easier to hold others responsible for my failures.

... people who feel they are in control of their lives are more internally focused; people who are feel in less control are more externally focused.

... that being aware of their beliefs provides the client with a choice about how they want to continue to believe.

... most people rely upon their non-serving beliefs.

Segment 5
I have observed that:

... that not making a decision is as much of a choice as making a decision.

...people are afraid of choices. Not having a choice is much easier than having to make a choice. Even if it's in your best interest.

Segment 6
I have observed that:

... opportunities come from the exploration of possibilities...not necessarily from ones first thought.

... some times your first thought is your best thought....even after the exploration.

Segment 7
I have observed that:

... I've been impressed with the out of the box thoughts that clients have come up with.

... balance is not all it's cracked up to be. I've observed that someone in balance doesn't move forward. Imbalance/dissatisfaction is what makes people change.

Segment 8

I have observed that:

… when time and actions are written they are more likely to happen.

… this is the segment that scares people. Writing a plan makes you more accountable to doing that plan….and being successful scares people more than a rationalized failure.

Segment 9

I have observed that:

… show me the money!!

… and lots of it!! And because of ME!!

Segment 10

I have observed that:

… commitment is easy when the payoff is bigger than the effort.

… it's time to "poo" or get off the pot.

Segment 11

I have observed that:

… people love to tell about their successes and they squirm in telling their failures.

… if you want to double your successes, double your failures. Try faster.

PACE AND TIMING

There are two aspects of coaching that differentiate coaching from good coaching. Pace and Timing.

First, pace. Pace is the skill demonstrated by a coach which moves the client through the coaching conversation in a timely manner. This implies that by the end of a session a suitable amount of information and questioning has been covered.

But, let's dig a little deeper. What is masterful pacing? The trick to masterful pacing is (1) following a consistent and reliable process and (2) CONSCIOUSLY being aware of where you are in the process and moving forward in a manner consistent with the needs of the client.....NOT the style of the coach.

Masterful pacing is a blend of moving the client toward action....at their speed.

Now, timing. Timing is the skill demonstrated by a coach to ask a question....at the right time.

But, again, let's go a little deeper. What is masterful timing? The trick to masterful timing is (1) asking the perfect question (2) at the perfect time and (3) for the perfect reason.

Therefore.....masterful pacing depends on a universal and reliable methodology. The CCS™ process provides that methodology.

Masterful timing depends on the perfect question, at the perfect time for the perfect reason. The CCS™ process provides a model for which question to ask and when to ask it. Whether the question is perfect, well, that's up to you!!

A COACHING CONVERSATION

The Conversation Chapter is designed to demonstrate the use of questions within the various segments and how to move the client through the model.

The purpose of this exercise is not to demonstrate the perfect coaching conversation or the use of advanced coaching skills taught by the various schools. Rather this exercise will be used to illustrate a single thread of conversation through the process...providing examples of questions derived from the Q-Tips...moving the client from the input to the output of each segment.

The conversation is broken up by segments within a table. The tables are divided into three columns. The first column identifies the speaker within that row, the coach (CO) or the client (CL).

The second column represents the conversation by that speaker. It should be noticed that the questions are derived from the Q-Tip and are not required to be verbatim from the book.

The third column represents the question or a comment about the example conversation.

Segment 1: Want		
CO:	So, what shall we talk about today?	Q-tip #1
CL:	My husband and I seem to argue about money a lot lately.	
CO:	Tell me more about your relationship with your husband.	Q-tip #3
CL:	The relationship is pretty good....we have our normal ups and downs; but money seems to be the cause of most of the arguments.	

CO:	Do you argue about anything else on a regular basis?	Q-tip #3
CL:	Well, we argue about the kids once in a while...he's more strict about school work than I am.	
CO:	So, how do you feel about arguing with your husband?	Q-tip #3
CL:	I HATE arguing ...it's so draining.	
CO:	Ok, so tell me...what do you really want?	Q-tip #10
CL:	I want to argue less with my husband about money.	Input
CO:	Is arguing about money more of an issue than arguing about the kids?	Q-tip #12
CL:	Definitely	
CO:	So, would you like to work on the issue of arguing less with your husband about money?	Output
CL:	Yes, that would be a good use of our time today.	

Segment 2: Motivation Conversation		
CO:	So, is arguing the issue or is arguing about money the issue?	Q-tip #1

CL:	Frankly, it's about the money. Things are so tight. We can barely breathe between paychecks.	Input
CO:	If nothing changes, what happens?	Q-tip #5
CL:	We will continue arguing…and things will just get worse.	
CO:	Do you have a budget; are you sticking to it?	Q-tip #6
CL:	We have a pretty good budget; but the smallest expense causes our budget to be stretched too tightly.	
CO:	So, if you get more money, will that solve your problems?	Q-tip #3
CL:	(laughs) Yes, if we had more money, life in general would be easier…and it would stop a lot of the arguing.	
CO:	Would having more money make you happier?	Q-tip #8
CL:	Of course, it would make life easier and eliminate arguing about money at least.	
CO:	So, should we talk about how you might get more money today?	Summary & Output
CL:	Sounds great.	

Segment 3: Issues Conversation		
CO:	So, how might you get more money?	Q-tip #1 & Input
CL:	Well, I can't imagine cutting our expenses any more. We have a tight budget and we stick to it.	

CL:	My husband works for XX Company and is at the top of his pay range...and was recently promoted...and won't be expecting a pay raise any time soon. It sure would be easier if he made more money, but I don't see that happening. (the story)	
CO:	What other alternatives can you think of to bring in more money?	Q-tip #7
CL:	Well, I can't take on another job, there just aren't enough hours in the day. So, I need to be making more money at the job I have. It sure would be easier if he just made more money. (second use of the story)	Story
CO:	You've already told me where the money CAN'T come from...the question is...where CAN it come from. (short circuiting the story; first attempt to stop the story)	Q-tip #4
CL:	Hmmm, since it can't come from him, I feel it will need to come from me. (sigh, not happy)	Output

Segment 4: Current View Conversation		
CO:	So, how could you come up with additional money?	Q-tip #1 & Input
CL:	Since I don't have more hours to work, I need to make more money per hour.	
CO:	What options can you think of?	Q-tip #1
CL:	Well, I could stay at my current job and make more...or change jobs and hope to get paid more.	
CO:	Let's talk about these alternatives briefly; what do you think about changing jobs?	Q-tip #3

CL:	The location of my current job is good; it's close to daycare, and our house is close to where I currently work. And I like the job and the people I work with.	
CO:	Changing jobs doesn't sound like it appeals to you....tell me more about your current job.	Q-tip #1
CL:	I like my job...I think I'm good at it...but I think I could take on more responsibility that might give me more income.	
CO:	Is there opportunity to get that responsibility...and more income?	Q-tip #2
CL:	I think so, but I'm not sure. I get normal pay raises, but I haven't been promoted in quite a while.	
CO:	Are you promotable?	Q-tip #5
CL:	I think I am....but I'm not sure my boss does. The last two promotions went to younger, but less experienced women. One person was even from another department.	Non serving belief
CO:	What do you think is stopping your boss from promoting YOU?	Q-tip #5
CL:	I never said that I've applied for the promotion...I just noticed who the promotions go to.	
CO:	How would you feel about going up for a promotion?	Q-tip #7
CL:	I feel nervous, because if I didn't get it.. it would be embarassing to have a younger, less experienced woman get the promotion instead of me.	Non serving belief

141

CL:	Then I'd get angry, probably quit my job…..then I'd have REAL money problems.	

(Coaching Note: Statements about the appearance of other candidates for promotion and her anger both lead to environmental issues of emotions and self-image.)

CO:	I've heard you say that emotions that come up for you regarding asking for a promotion. And that you have observed that a younger, more attractive person seems to get the job. I hear you say that you would be embarrassed if someone prettier got the job. And that embarrassment makes you angry. Is that true?	Q-tip #6 Restatement of a potential story and non serving belief
CL:	Sadly, yes.	
CO:	Have you ever been promoted at this company? Why?	Q-tip #1
CL:	No, I've only been here for three years….however, after 2 years many of my colleagues have been promoted already.	
CO:	Have you ever been promoted at any company you've worked for?	Q-tip #1
CL:	I was promoted twice at the last company I worked for.	
CO:	What did you have to do to get that promotion? What did you learn that might be applicable here?	Q-tip #9

CL:	I worked hard...I worked a lot of hours...and I made my boss look good whenever I could.	
CO:	Have you ever been passed over for a promotion? Why?	Q-tip #1 & 9
CL:	Not at my former company. Here, well, I've never really told anyone that I wanted to be promoted. I just assumed that if I worked hard enough, my boss would see what I was doing and promote me without having to ask.	
CO:	Could there be any other reason that you haven't been promoted...other than the looks of another person?	Q-tip #6
CL:	Not that I can think of. I'm not sure how they got their promotion.	
CO:	What have you done to let your boss know that you were interested in being promoted?	Q-tip #10
CL:	Well, to be honest, not much.	
CO:	Ok, so, how has being angry and embarrassed worked for you?	Q-tip #10
CL:	Not very well....and it exhausts me.	
CO:	All of that being said......Who is responsible for your promotability?	Q-tip #5
CL:	I guess my ability to get promoted is more up to me. I guess being embarrassed and angry doesn't help me get a promotion and **I need to be responsible for my own promotability**.	Output & **Key Statement**

	Segment 5: Choices Conversation	
CO	So you believe that getting promoted is up to you?	Summary & Input
CL	Yes, I do.	
CO:	What are you feeling right now?	Q-tip #3
CL:	I'm exhausted; I'm spending too much time not getting anything done....and I'm angry that I'm not getting promoted...even if it is my fault.	
CO:	How would you feel about getting rid of that anger and embarrassment?	Q-tip #3
CL:	It would be wonderful. I'd sleep better, my husband would certainly be happier...and I'd be happier at work.	
CO:	How would being promoted...and the money that comes with the promotion...make you feel?	Q-tip #3
CL:	Well, it would certainly make it more fun to work and the extra money would really help.	
CO:	Could you survive being turned down the first time you try for a promotion?	Q-tip #6
CL:	Hmm, that might be pretty devastating...especially the first time.	
CO:	But, how about if together we built a support system to help you try...and survive...either way.	Q-tip #7
CL:	Now that might work...sure.	
CO:	Do you have the energy right now to do what it might take to get promoted?	Q-tip #7

CL:	It's sounding like I should try….and my husband would love it.	
CO:	Are you willing to make that change?	Q-tip #7 & Output
CL:	I'm willing to give it a good try.	

	Segment 6: Future View Conversation	
CO	Great, it's good to make a choice.	Summary & Input
CL	Yes, I'm ready to continue	
CO:	What are the priorities? It seems like we have talked about embarrassment and anger; but we haven't talked much about your self image and promotability. Is that what you think?	Q-tip #1
CL:	I think that my self image could use some work; I'm ok with how I look but I'm not as young as I used to be…but I'm ok with my appearance.	
CO:	Do you think your appearance affects your promotability?	Q-tip #5
CL:	Probably to some small extent, but on the other hand, my experience should be enough to overcome any appearance issues.	
CO:	So, then…..what DO you think might improve your chances of being promoted?	Q-tip #8
CL:	Well, I need to start seriously thinking about how to be promoted and I need to start feeling like I deserve to be promoted.	
CO:	What might help you feel like you deserve to be promoted?	Q-tip #2 & 7
CL:	Well, I certainly need to figure out what my boss needs…in order to promote me. If there are any skills, responsibilities…anything…that I	

	should be doing to be the best candidate for the next promotion.	
CO:	So, what have you learned from what you've just said?	Q-tip #9
CL:	I need to figure out how to feel like the perfect candidate for the next, appropriate promotion.	Summary & Output
CO:	So, that would make you feel like you were promotable?	
CL:	Yes, I believe so.	

Segment 7: Force Analysis Conversation		
CO:	Now, let's talk about what would support or resist your being the perfect candidate? Let's start with the support that you have. So, what would make you feel like you were promotable?	Input & Q-tip #1
CL:	Well, my husband supports me.	
CL:	The people I work with would have no problem with my being promoted; a couple have even indicated that they would support me in trying to be promoted.	
CO:	That sounds pretty good. And, what about you.....are you up for this?	Q-tip #4
CL:	Yes, I'm definitely ready...it's time for me to get on with this.	
CO:	That all sounds very good. Now, is there anyone or anything that might get in your way....that might be a resisting influence?	Q-tip #5
CL:	Well, I'm not really sure about how my boss feels about promoting me. He could go either way, I'm just not sure where he stands.	

CO:	Ok, is there anything else?	Q-tip #6
CL:	There is one thing; many of the previous candidates had....leadership training. That might be something that would help.	
CO:	Now for the hard question.....asking for the promotion. Does asking for the promotion still feel like an obstacle?	Q-tip #10
CL:	Yes....that's probably the toughest thing. But, I feel that all of this conversation has made some of the issues less than it was when we started...but, it's not going to be easy.	
CO:	Well, we've covered a lot of area; can you pull it all together, can you summarize what you've just said?	Summary
CL:	Ok, there are three obstacles that I need to handle and three supports that I can rely on to help me. They are:	Output

Obstacles	Support
Me, asking for the promotion. My leadership training. Knowledge of what my boss thinks of my promotability.	I'm motivated...it's time. My husband is all for my additional income. My colleagues are supportive.

Segment 8: Action Plan Conversation		
CO:	Ok, that sounds like a pretty good list of obstacles and supports, doesn't it?	Input
CL:	Yes, I think it's a pretty good list.	
CO:	Great. One of the techniques which has worked well with others is to brainstorm a list of all of the activities which would accommodate your obstacles and maximize your support. Sound ok?	Q-tip #1 & 5

CL:	Sure, let's do it.	
CO:	What do you think needs to be done to get you promoted?	Q-tip #2
CL:	Brainstormed List of Actions: (discussion facilitated by coach...but all of the client's ideas. These tasks are in no particular order...straight from the client.)	

1. Ask for the promotion

2. Find out from boss if he would support a promotion

3. Ask boss if there are any additional skills that are necessary prior to promotion

4. Ask supportive colleagues if they know of anything I should be doing.

5. Share with husband intention to ask for the promotion; discuss implications

6. Develop a strategy for asking for the promotion.

7. Contact people who have been promoted; maybe get a mentor/champion from one of them

8. Talk to my HR person to see if there are any administrative issues that need to be managed; maybe other opportunities within the company.

9. Ask HR representative if there is any training that is available to make you more acceptable for future promotion.

10. Develop a strategy in the event that a promotion is not going to happen within the foreseeable future.

CO:	That's a great list....you've obviously given this a lot of thought. Now, which of these tasks do you think are the most important....let's make a list of those priorities.	Q-tip #3

Coach Note: At this point, the Coach and the Client spend a significant amount of time grouping together and prioritizing the task list. This list will not be provided here, but will be transferred into the ACTION PLAN table below.

CO:	So, are these the actions, in priority, that you need to take to get your promotion?	Q-tip #3
CL:	Yes, I have the list of all actions that I need to take and I agree with the priority of those tasks.	
CO:	Now, we need to convert that list into an action plan. The way that I typically construct an action plan is by using the ACTION PLAN format document I've provided you with. Why don't we work together to convert the actions you have indicated into an action plan? Sound ok with you? (See attached Action Plan in Appendix A)	Q-tip #8 & Output
CL:	Sounds good…let's do it!!	

Coach Note: Below is the ACTION PLAN document that was developed with the Client and the Coach.

The action list has been prioritized and sequenced. Then, the client and coach developed the subaction steps required to accomplish the action. Then, finally, the list was put into the ACTION PLAN format.

Below you will see the abbreviated Action Plan. This abbreviated document was done merely to save space. For the full Action Plan, see Appendix A.

WANT: Get a Promotion		Today's Date: 09-02-09	
Priority	**Action/Subaction**	**Anticipated Completion Date**	**Actual Completion Date**
I	Share with husband intention to ask for the promotion; discuss implications a. Talk about what you want to do b. Discuss how it might impact the family c. Ask if he's ok with pursuing the promotion	(examples) 09-02-09	
2	Ask supportive colleagues if they know of anything I should be doing. a. Identify who you should talk with b. Ask the colleague if they think you are ready for a promotion c. Can they think of anything I should be doing to prepare for a promotion	09-05-09	
3	Talk to my HR friend a. -----------	09-12-09	

Segment 9: Verify Payoff Conversation		
CO:	Ok, you have the completed action plan...now we need talk about the payoff for going through all of this planning and effort. What will you personally get out of going through all of this?	Input & Q-tip #1
CL:	What I'm getting out of all of this effort is that, in the event that I get a promotion, my husband and I will be arguing less and our financial situation will be better. And I feel very confident and much more powerful than when we first started this conversation.	Output #1

CO:	How will you handle NOT getting the promotion in spite of your hard work?	Q-tip #12
CL:	Even if I don't get the promotion, I'll have an insight in what other options might be available to me.	Output #2
CO:	When you get the promotion, how will your husband feel?	Q-tip #7
CL:	He'll be very proud; he'll see that I've worked hard...and got what I worked so hard for. And, assuming I got the promotion, it will take a lot of pressure off of him about money. I know it's keeping him up at night. He'll definitely feel more relaxed.	Output #3

Segment 10: Commitment Conversation		
CO:	Do you trust the action plan...the strategy you've constructed?	Q-tip #2
CL:	Yes, it seems pretty thorough.	
CO:	Are the payoffs clear? Do you know why you are going through all of this?	Input & Q-tip #3
CL:	Yes, I'm actually getting excited about doing all of this.	
CO:	Are you ready to start?	Q-tip #8
CL:	Yes, I'm ready to start. The plan looks good. It's got what I need to do. The tasks are broken into small enough, bite sized pieces. I really believe I can do this!!	Output #1
CO:	It sounds like you are ready to take action. Is there anything else we need to talk about before we end this session?	Q-tip #7

CL:	No, I'm ready to go!	Output #2
CO:	Great, then I'll talk to you during our next session. You've worked hard today and I think you did a great job in keeping focused on exactly what you wanted. I'll be looking forward to getting feedback from you about how you did on those tasks which you've committed to by our next session.	Concluding statements
CL:	Great; I'll talk to you then	

Coaching Note: At this point, conclude the conversation. Begin the next session/conversation with the Feedback segment, then move on to the Want segment to complete the concentric conversation.

Segment 11: Feedback Conversation		
CO:	Welcome back. You were very excited about starting your action plan when we last spoke; how did things go?	Input & Q-tip #1
CL:	Thanks....I have a lot to tell you about.	
CO:	Wonderful; so, what would you like to tell me?	Q-tip #2 & 4
CL:	Well, a couple of things have happened this week......	
The results of this question will be the basis for the input to the Want segment input.		
CO:	Ok, good job....so, what do you want to do next?	Output & Q-tip #7

Coaching Note: At this point, a new concentric cycle is initiated. The coach should listen carefully to what the client has to say. The client is expected to report on what they did during the time between sessions and their progress toward completing their action plan.

Be aware that the client may have experienced a change in circumstances and may bring a new want to the conversation.

Don't forget; the conversation is about the client....not what you expect of the client!!

For those of you who were curious about the outcome of the coaching for this young woman, she did NOT get the promotion. However, another manager saw her skillful preparation for the promotion, heard that she was actually so interested in her job that she hired her own coach...and the other manager hired her. Now she is making more money, loves her new job, and her relationship with her husband is moving toward a new and richer part of their lives.

DO'S AND DON'TS

DO..............Encourage your client to be honest. To say what they
feel needs to be said, even if they don't know what
they actually feel.

DON'T.........Encourage your client to hide behind their stories.

DO..............Handle separately the issues of meeting a goal versus
going deeper. Sometimes a client just wants to do
something concrete and not get into how they feel
about it.

DON'T.........Let a client ignore their feelings. Part of being a coach
is revealing the client to themselves. Explore
feelings...but keep it in perspective.

DO..............Keep checking with the client about each step in the
process. Coaching is about the client....not adhering
to YOUR process.

DON'T.........Forget that diminishing pain makes the client more
protected, but increasing joy enlarges the client.

DO..............Stick to the facts. Take into consideration the opinion
of both the client and their external environments; but,
ALWAYS rely on the facts.

DON'T.........Let a client dwell on their stories; take note of the
point of the story, maybe even catalog the story (if the
client is a relentless storyteller), and then short circuit
repetitive, non-serving stories.

DO..............Help the client construct a concrete key statement
defining their true want. Then, help the client
construct a clear, clean, concrete action statement.
You're 90% on your way to real success as a coach.

DON'T.........Short change the development of a <u>written</u> action plan. This process will often freak out a client because they realize if they make a written action plan...they actually have to do it...and they actually have to take the risk of failure. Or worse, actually succeeding.

DO.............Require clear feedback from all previous coaching sessions. If they can't tell you what they did...they probably didn't do it.

DON'T.........Confuse "not much to report back to you" with not doing anything. Some action plans take time. As the phrase goes, Rome wasn't built in a day, and relationships, plans, strategic development....all of this takes time. But an appropriate amount of time. Be appropriate.

Appendix A

THE COMPLETE ACTION PLAN

ACTION PLAN

WANT: Get a Promotion   **Today's Date: 09-02-09**

Priority	Action/Subaction	Anticipated Completion Date	Actual Completion Date
1	Share with husband intention to ask for the promotion; discuss implications d. Talk about what you want to do e. Discuss how it might impact the family f. Ask if he's ok with pursuing the promotion	(examples) 09-02-09	
2	Ask supportive colleagues if they know of anything I should be doing. d. Identify who you should talk with e. Ask the colleague if they think you are ready for a promotion f. Can they think of anything I should be doing to prepare for a promotion	09-05-09	

	ACTION PLAN (Continued)		
3	Talk to my HR friend b. Ask if there are there any administrative issues that need to be managed c. Ask if there is there any training that I should take to make me more acceptable for future promotion d. Ask if there is anything else I should be doing to be more promotable.	09-12-09	
4	Contact people who have been promoted; maybe get a mentor/champion from one of them a. Identify a previously promoted person who might be willing to talk confidentially about what it took to get promoted b. Make an appointment with that person c. Ask what it took them to be promoted	(to be continued)	
5	Develop a strategy for asking for the promotion. a. Put together what I think I might want to do to prepare for a meeting to discuss a possible promotion b. Select someone who might dispassionately review my strategy with me c. Make the appropriate revisions to my strategy. d. Repeat until I am comfortable with my strategy		

	ACTION PLAN (Continued)		
6	Develop a strategy in the event that a promotion is not going to happen within the foreseeable future. a. Pick a friend/spouse who would be willing to speak frankly with me about the possibility of not getting the promotion. b. Explore with that person the possibility of working in another department, group or even another company. c. Spend some time exploring how I feel about leaving my current job.		
7	Find out from boss if he would support a promotion; Ask boss if there are any additional skills that are necessary prior to promotion a. Make an appointment with my boss to discuss the possibilities of promotion b. List what I'd like to discuss with my boss on 3x5 cards. c. If time permits, role play a possible discussion with a trusted colleague or friend.		
8	Ask for the promotion a. Identify a promotion opportunity that would perfectly suit my skills and abilities b. Schedule a meeting with my boss to discuss an actual promotion. c. Identify all of the attributes, skills, and experience that would make me the perfect candidate for that position…and why promoting me would be a good choice by the boss.		

ORDER FORM

First, I would like to thank you for purchasing, and hopefully using, *The Concentric Coaching System: A Systematic Coaching Model*™ book. I hope that it has been as valuable a tool to you as it has been in my own practice.

As you find yourself using the techniques described in the book, you may be interested our other product offerings including:

CCS SYSTEM™ a discounted package of all the **CCS**™ product offerings

CCS MAP™ a full color 8.5 x 14 inch laminated Map

CCS *Question at a Glance*™ Guidebook to aid you in identifying, selecting, and remembering the perfect question.

CCS Coach Workbook™ Coaches Workbook

CCS Client Workbook™

CCS Coaching Hours Log™

CCS Environment Scan Card™

CCS Workbook™ refills

If you would like to order other product(s), please do one of the following:

1. Go to our website at www.Myriad-PSI.com

2. If you feel like talking or ordering an obscene number of the books, guidebooks, or **MAP**™s, please contact:

   Brian P. O'Brien at 301-682-8382, Brian@Myriad-PSI.com

Thanks for your support.

Sincerely,

Brian P. O'Brien

www.ingramcontent.com/pod-product-compliance
Lightning Source LLC
Chambersburg PA
CBHW051525170526
45165CB00002B/604